COMMITMENT TO OBEDIENCE

ELIZABETH NAPIER

SAVED IN CHRIST PUBLICATIONS

Commitment to Obedience

Published in Carleton, MI by Saved in Christ Publications. For fundraising opportunities, wholesale purchase, or educational use please email savedsisterinchrist@gmail.com.

ISBN: 979-8-9881040-4-9
Library of Congress Control Number: 2024920395

Cover and interior design: Elizabeth Napier. Cover Images by Dimitrisvetsikas1969 from Pixabay.

1 2 3 4 5 6 7 8 9 10

Almighty Father,
Thank you.
For everything.

Table of Contents

1

Introduction

"But ask the animals now, and they will teach you; the birds of the sky, and they will tell you. Or speak to the earth, and it will teach you. The fish of the sea will declare to you."

- Job 12:7-8

"Blessed is everyone who fears Yahweh, who walks in his ways. For you will eat the labor of your hands. You will be happy, and it will be well with you."

- Psalm 128:1

"The world is passing away with its lusts, but he who does God's will remains forever."

- 1 John 2:17

"Peace! Be still!" Those are some valuable words when it comes to understanding obedience, on so many levels. They are spoken by Jesus, in Mark 4:37-40, as He and the disciples are crossing the Sea of Galilee:

> A big wind storm arose, and the waves beat into the boat, so much that the boat was already filled. He himself was in the stern, asleep on the cushion; and they woke him up and asked him, "Teacher, don't you care that we are dying?" He awoke and rebuked the wind, and said to the sea, "Peace! Be still!" The wind ceased and there was a great calm. He said to them, "Why are you so afraid? How is it that you have no faith?" They were greatly afraid and said to one another, "Who then is this, that even the wind and the sea obey him?"

After everything they have seen so far, the disciples are shocked to realize that nature obeys Jesus. We can also realize a few things from this example. One, is how the wind and sea obeyed His command: instantly, and without question. They both ceased to blow and rage as soon as Jesus spoke the words, "Peace! Be still!" They did not argue with Him, or question Him, asking, 'Why should we stop?' They didn't ask for five more minutes to storm. They simply stopped.

Imagine if your toddler obeyed you that quickly and easily! Imagine if we all were as obedient to the Lord as the wind and sea. Truly, it is not shocking that nature obeys Him. What is more shocking, is that we do not. God designed every living and non-living thing on Earth to obey His commands. Controlling the waves and wind is easy. It is only us humans who have a difficult time being obedient to God, because of our free-will.

The obedience of nature can be a good model for us to follow. The examples of nature's obedience in the Bible are designed by God to show us how we should obey Him, and, in at least one instance, what could happen if we do not. We are soldiers in the battle against the principalities and powers of darkness at work in this world. We made the choice to serve the Most High God, Creator of the heavens and earth, of all that is, seen and unseen. We have been tested by some fiery trials, and have been learning how to walk in His ways. We have invited the Holy Spirit to fill us, and sanctify us, until we are made pure and holy. Now, we must learn how to steadfastly obey Him, as soldiers obey their commander.

God created you. He is your Creator. He gave you the capacity to do everything that He expects you to do. All you have to do is have real faith that you will be successful, or He would not have called upon you to do it. If you trust and listen, He will teach you what you need to know, and build you up for what He wants you to do. We are part of His kingdom now. We are His servants, His hands, and His feet. We work for Him. It is our duty to see that God's will is done here on Earth, by us, just as those in Heaven obey His will.

Why does God wait for us to do things, instead of just doing them Himself? Why does God give us commands? Why does He want our help? When I was washing the dishes one day, I carefully cleaned a beautiful glass teacup my children had bought me for a Mother's Day gift. It started me thinking about how I could easily have purchased any teacup I wanted for myself. I also had other mugs and cups in the cabinet, so I did not *need* them to buy me the teacup. Then I thought about the school crafts young children lovingly make for their families, or when they try to help make dinner. Surely their parents could draw better pictures, or cook better meals, but that isn't the point. Doing so would deprive all of us of joy, them of the opportunity to give their parents a gift, and us parents of receiving a gift from our children. It also allows the children to learn.

God is the same, when He asks us to do tasks He could clearly accomplish without our help. He does this, at least in part, to allow us the joy of helping Him. We receive the privilege of participating in God's works. It is a chance to show we love Him, and have faith in Him. We should be thrilled that He has chosen us and given us the opportunity. In addition, God also wants us to learn, to make sure our faith is strong enough to endure through every storm. Sometimes the tasks He gives us are challenges that will help us strengthen and test our faith. They may teach us, or someone else, a lesson. Sometimes He wants things done for His purposes, and as His servants, we just have to do them. Like receiving orders from a military officer, information may be given on a need-to-know basis. We do not always need to know why God is telling us to do something, we just need to be obedient, and trust Him.

What exactly does it mean to be obedient? When we read the Bible, we discover that obedience consists of several components, and is displayed in various forms. These all originate from the same place: the Holy Spirit living within you and attuning you to God's voice. The Holy Spirit makes you aware of the Lord's commands, and helps you to understand them. The components and forms of obedience include: belief and repentance, commitment, the biblical Commandments, practice of the spiritual disciplines, being the church, the Great Commission, having an answer for your faith, humility, and direct orders.

The initial four components were the subjects of the first three books in this series, so we will just briefly recap them in this introduction. They build the base of our faith, making these other forms of obedience possible. We will then spend the remainder of this book focusing on each of the other forms of obedience, as well as looking at some examples of disobedience. We will learn about the types of people God uses, the kinds of tasks He asks people to perform, and what the various types of obedience look like in practice.

Let's begin our review with the most obvious foundational component, belief and repentance. Clearly we must at first believe in God, and in our redemption by Jesus Christ, in order to be obedient to God. If we do not even believe God exists, then why would we need to obey Him? Belief is defined as, "an acceptance that a statement is true or that something exists" or "confidence in the truth or existence of something not immediately susceptible to rigorous proof". Belief in anything is a choice we make, and each of us must determine for ourselves if we believe in God's existence, Jesus's sacrifice, and the teachings of the Bible.

In *Logic to Belief*, we discuss a few logical reasons for believing in God, and in all of these books, we work on investigating and deepening our belief. We learned about the impacts of our sinfulness, and the importance of repentance. We have to love God, and hate our sin. We have to ask Him to set us free from the chains of our sin. Part of our faithful obedience means we agree that our sins are wrong, and we ask for His help to stop sinning.

You can know for certain that God is real, that Christ died to save us, and you can be filled with the Holy Spirit. You must simply seek Him, repent, and receive His forgiveness. Then ask to be filled with, and cleansed by, the Holy Spirit. Since this is now book four, I will assume you already have a belief in God, and that you have already begun taking the steps to build a solid relationship with Him. If not, please know that you can, and must, have your own personal relationship with Him. If you seek after Him with your whole heart, body, and mind, you will find Him.

In fact, the God of Abraham is the only God who encourages and wants every single human to talk with Him. Every other religion reserves the ability to hear their gods for a select group, or certain prophets, if they even allow humans to talk to their gods at all. This is because their gods are not real. You cannot talk with someone who isn't real, they would not answer back. Our God is real, which is why everyone can talk to Him, and have their own relationship with Him. You can hear His voice, if you are listening for it.

Next, let's quickly cover the components of commitment, God's Commandments, and the practice of the spiritual disciplines. In *Belief to Pursuit*, we explored the Commandments, as well as some of the spiritual disciplines. In *Pursuit to Commitment*, we spent more time on the spiritual disciplines. We also learned about committing and surrendering our lives completely to God. We discussed the truth that all people have broken God's laws, and fallen short of obedience to His Commandments. This is why we needed the Messiah to save our souls by purchasing them from death. Although we could not purchase our own salvation, we read throughout the Bible that we are still responsible for, and can be judged for, the choices we make. We learned that if we love Jesus, and invite the Holy Spirit to live within us, He helps us reject the sins of our flesh. We naturally desire to obey His Commandments, because we see how disobeying them hurts people. We also learned that we must keep our faith strong through constant immersion in the spiritual disciplines of prayer, worship, tithing, fasting, serving, and reading the Bible. Without building a strong foundation in Christ through obedience to these basic components, we leave ourselves vulnerable to attack.

We delved into learning about our commitment to the sanctification process, and how Jesus gives us freedom from the bondage of our sins. When we commit to that process, we are allowing the Holy Spirit to make ourselves into purified vessels that can be used by God. We learn how to stop giving our lives over to the pursuit of sin and worldly desires. In

Matthew 18:8-9, Jesus cautions us to do whatever it takes to stop practicing sinful behavior:

> If your hand or your foot causes you to stumble, cut it off and cast it from you. It is better for you to enter into life maimed or crippled, rather than having two hands or two feet to be cast into the eternal fire. If your eye causes you to stumble, pluck it out and cast it from you. It is better for you to enter into life with one eye, rather than having two eyes to be cast into the Gehenna of fire.

At times, people are likened to vessels, as in Jeremiah 18:3-6:

> Then I went down to the potter's house, and behold, he was making something on the wheels. When the vessel that he made of the clay was marred in the hand of the potter, he made it again another vessel, as seemed good to the potter to make it. Then Yahweh's word came to me, saying, "House of Israel, can't I do with you as this potter?" says Yahweh. "Behold, as the clay in the potter's hand, so are you in my hand, house of Israel.

In order to be found suitable for the Lord's work, we have to be available, and go through His training program, which we discussed more thoroughly in *Pursuit to Commitment*. We must allow the Holy Spirit to help us grow and change from within. Have you allowed Him to remake you into a suitable vessel, or do you resist the Potter's hands and the fire of sanctification? Have you allowed the Holy Spirit to prepare you to be usable? Are you willing to be purified, cleansed of your sinfulness, and completely give up the things of this world?

Our bodies are vessels. God cannot pour good and holy things into unclean and unsuitable vessels. Every vessel is meant to hold something, and ours can either hold evil, or the

Holy Spirit. You would not serve your Sunday dinner out of vessels like your car's dirty oil pan, or your cat's litter box. Neither can our dirty selves serve God's purposes. We must first submit to the sanctification process to allow our souls and minds to be cleansed, so we are refined into appropriate vessels to serve our King. This process teaches us how to obey His commands and be made holy.

An important step in our sanctification, is learning how to forgive every single offense that people commit toward us. After all, we are rejoicing in the Lord's forgiveness of our own sins, even though they were many. We should extend that same mercy and forgiveness to the actions of our fellow servants against ourselves. Jesus explains this in a parable:

> Then Peter came and said to him, "Lord, how often shall my brother sin against me, and I forgive him? Until seven times?" Jesus said to him, "I don't tell you until seven times, but, until seventy times seven. Therefore the Kingdom of Heaven is like a certain king who wanted to settle accounts with his servants. When he had begun to settle, one was brought to him who owed him ten thousand talents. But because he couldn't pay, his lord commanded him to be sold, with his wife, his children, and all that he had, and payment to be made. The servant therefore fell down and knelt before him, saying, 'Lord, have patience with me, and I will repay you all!' The lord of that servant, being moved with compassion, released him and forgave him the debt.
>
> But that servant went out and found one of his fellow servants who owed him one hundred denarii, and he grabbed him and took him by the throat, saying, 'Pay me what you owe!' So his fellow servant fell down at his

> feet and begged him, saying, 'Have patience with me, and I will repay you!' He would not, but went and cast him into prison until he should pay back that which was due. So when his fellow servants saw what was done, they were exceedingly sorry, and came and told their lord all that was done. Then his lord called him in and said to him, 'You wicked servant! I forgave you all that debt because you begged me. Shouldn't you also have had mercy on your fellow servant, even as I had mercy on you?' His lord was angry, and delivered him to the tormentors until he should pay all that was due to him. So my heavenly Father will also do to you, if you don't each forgive your brother from your hearts for his misdeeds." (Matthew 18:21-35)

To obey God, we must turn over our lives to God. We spent time in *Pursuit to Commitment* exploring what this looks like, so we will be fully prepared to complete whatever tasks He asks us to accomplish, and to work in obedience to His will. In order to serve Christ with our full heart, body, mind, and soul, we must be completely dedicated to that objective. We must be free from all other entanglements so that they do not get in the way of our serving the Lord. If we have too many other distractions, we end up putting Him on the back burner, and forgetting our obligations.

We have all become desperately attached to the things of this modern world. We work so hard just to pay our mortgages, car payments, credit cards, or student loans. We effectively become indentured servants to our bosses or customers in order to pay our debts. When we consistently chase after bigger and better things on Earth, we can become so busy that we ultimately miss out on the far greater rewards awaiting us in His eternal kingdom. When we focus on doing what we *think* is best, instead of giving that up to find out what God *knows* is best, it never quite works out in our favor. We spend all of our time, energy, health, and life serving our earthly desires, and rarely make time to serve the Lord.

Ask yourself if you are ready to work in obedience to His will. Are you entangled in worthless pursuits, or are you available to serve Christ in your life? There are 168 hours in one week. Track how you spend them. How many of them do you devote to the Lord? Does He get the most hours of your time, or the least? What is your ultimate objective in life? Is it to buy a bigger house, pay for your children to go to university, and save for retirement? Or is it to live and die for the Lord?

All of those practices make up the foundational components of our obedience to God's will. He expects us to believe in Him. He expects us to give our absolute commitment to Him alone, not dividing our loyalties between Him and the world. He expects us to repent and invite the Holy Spirit in, turn away from sin, and submit to sanctification. He expects us to keep His Commandments. He expects us to practice the spiritual disciplines regularly for the rest of our lives. Those actions make up the minimum requirements to obeying God. If we miss any of those components, we are outside of the will of God, and are not obeying Him. Thus, first things first: we have to ensure we are obeying these basics, as they will make it possible for us to obey God more fully and easily. It becomes much more likely you will be obedient to God in other ways, if you already have the firm foundation in Christ that these initial steps provide.

Finally, I must give my usual admonishments. Read the entire Bible for yourself, and continue to read it daily. This is so important. In addition to scripture being one of your best defenses against attacks, we learn in John 1:14, "The Word became flesh and lived among us. We saw his glory, such glory as of the only born Son of the Father, full of grace and truth." Jesus is the Word of God, so if you do not know the Word you do not know Jesus. Of course the converse is also true, if you do not know Jesus, you do not know the Word. We must know His Word and keep His Word:

> Jesus answered him, "If a man loves me, he will keep my word. My Father will love him, and we will come to him and make our home with him. He who doesn't love me doesn't keep my words. The word which you hear isn't mine, but the Father's who sent me. "I have said these things to you while still living with you. But the Counselor, the Holy Spirit, whom the Father will send in my name, will teach you all things, and will remind you of all that I said to you. (John 14:23-26)

If we don't know the Word, if we do not follow Him and keep our obedience to God's Word, we will not know the way to the Father. As Jesus said, "I am the way, the truth, and the life. No one comes to the Father, except through me. If you had known me, you would have known my Father also. From now on, you know him and have seen him." (John 14:6-7) If we do not know Jesus, if we do not know the Bible, and if we do not have the Holy Spirit, we will be lost.

As with all humans, I am not any type of sovereign authority. Please compare everything I, or any other people, say with the Word of God. Guard against false prophecy. Pray and talk to God about everything you hear and read. Ask Him if it is true. Look up what the Bible says on the topic and see if it lines up. Every human who writes or speaks about God is capable of making an error, so we must proceed with caution and know the Word ourselves.

I am not a perfect person. I make mistakes and I have sinned like everyone else. Please do not assume anything I write in these books is judgment from me. I am simply trying to share what I have learned, in the hopes it helps someone else. I aim to share enough about my own sins in these books to help people realize that it is OK, and in fact, necessary, to admit you have sinned. Writing these books has helped me to recognize my own transgressions, and opened me up so I would allow the Holy Spirit to dig out their roots. We all need the help of the Holy Spirit to learn and be cleansed. I am the first to admit that I do not do all of the activities outlined in these books perfectly, but I am seeking His help to do more, and become better, each day. Your walk with God will have natural ebbs and flows. You will experience both calm and stormy seas. Stick it out, stay the course. Remember that Jesus is, has been, and always will be in the boat with you. God loves you, and you can trust that it will all work out in the end, the way He intends it to.

Most importantly, I pray this book supports your own obedience. We must stick together as soldiers on God's side in this war for humanity. Ultimately, we must remember that there is nothing we can do to be saved, other than to choose to repent and return to God, accept the Holy Spirit, and follow Christ. We could never afford the price to free our souls from death, so Jesus paid it for us. Now our job is to seek the Lord, get to know the Lord, and share the Lord. We could never do enough good on our own to cancel out the bad we have done. We could never be obedient enough to be perfect. We could never follow all of the laws well enough to save ourselves. We all need the sacrifice of Jesus, and the Holy Spirit to live within us, so we can be cleansed of our desire for sin. We all need to seek Him, know Him, and share Him so that others can realize they too have been saved, and accept their own salvation.

Heavenly Father,

All honor and glory belong to You. Please inventory our hearts, minds, and souls to remove anything that is not pleasing to You. Sanctify us and make us clean vessels, ready to do Your work. Help us to be humble and gracious servants as we seek to know Your will for our lives. Thank You for giving us the knowledge and ability to overcome the doubt and fear that tries to stop us from being obedient to You. We are grateful for the sacrifice of Jesus Christ to save us, and for the Holy Spirit working within us. Please help us to hear, understand, and obey You. Make Your voice clear and give us the strength to persevere in obedience to Your will. We ask this in the name of Your Son, our Savior, Jesus Christ.

Amen.

Notes

2

CHOSEN BY GOD

"You are my friends if you do whatever I command you. No longer do I call you servants, for the servant doesn't know what his lord does. But I have called you friends, for everything that I heard from my Father, I have made known to you. You didn't choose me, but I chose you and appointed you, that you should go and bear fruit, and that your fruit should remain; that whatever you will ask of the Father in my name, he may give it to you. "I command these things to you, that you may love one another."

- John 15:14-17

Do you remember those 'Uncle Sam wants you!' posters with the picture of him pointing at you? That is basically God's recruitment statement: He wants you! No matter who you are, or what you have done, He wants you. No matter how little you think you know, or how unskilled you think you are, God wants you working for Him. He has a plan for your life. All you have to do to find out His plan, is surrender to Him, and follow Him with your whole heart. You are already loved and chosen by Him. You have committed to walking across the line in the sand, and to giving up everything you left behind on the other side. It sounds relatively simple sometimes, but as we see in biblical examples, and in our own experiences, it is a lot more difficult in practice.

One thing that stood out to me when I began studying God's Word, is how awful most of the people were. I was expecting the main figures in the Bible to be these righteous, holy, shining examples of relative sinlessness, something we could all aspire to be. I assumed that if a beloved 'hero of the faith' said or did something, then their words and actions must be condoned by God. Some of them seemed to hold up to that reputation: Daniel, Enoch, and Job come to mind. However, as I read, I learned that the overwhelming majority did some very scandalous things. At first I was confused and upset that their vile behavior often seemed to be overlooked by God. How could He choose such terrible people?

Eventually, I realized that they, like all of us, were only human, and were just as susceptible to the enemy's temptations as we are. They believed in God, but their faith was tested just as ours is. They were weak, they made mistakes, they took matters into their own hands instead of waiting for God. They had doubts and fears, which led to them doing some bad things. They were real, flawed, sinful people. The wonderful thing about that, and the reason the Bible makes a point of sharing all of those embarrassing, terrible details about their lives, is that it gives the rest of us hope that we can also be forgiven. We can also be found acceptable to God. If people as sinful and awful as they were can be found worthy to serve Him, then we can too. We do not have to be perfect before God will choose us. He has chosen to save all who are willing to accept salvation.

If God is not looking for perfection and power, then what is He looking for? When hiring someone for a job, we usually want to know more about a person than what they look like. We tend to have a general profile of a perfect candidate in mind, and look for someone who fits. Do they have the right experience or training? Do they have the proper credentials? Are they a good match for the company or project? We may even do a background check, depending on the type of job. Interestingly, those chosen by God do not usually fit the profile we might expect. He often overlooks the wealthy, seemingly religious, famous, powerful, or strong, to choose the outcasts and the powerless. He does this because God sees what we cannot. When we conduct background checks, or search a prospective candidate's social media profiles, we are trying to look deeper than the surface. We are seeking more detailed information than what we can glean from an interview or resume.

If God simply looked at outward appearances, it would be easy to find people who look the part. Perhaps it is the church member who is there for every event, active socially in the church, and serving on all the committees. They seem to be devoting themselves to the Lord, but if we could see beneath the surface, we might find they are really doing all of this work to serve their own pride, and glorify themselves. They yearn for people to recognize their effort and sacrifices, and to see them as a martyr, or some sort of super-Christian. They want to seem popular and connected to everything, and everyone, at the church. They might be friendly in public, but then gossip and complain about the members who don't do as much, or as well, as they do. They may spread rumors based on what others have told them in confidence. Unfortunately, this type of vain 'religious' work is not how we are to love our neighbors, as commanded by Christ, "This is my commandment, that you love one another, even as I have loved you." (John 15:12)

God does not see us as the image we present to everyone else. As we learn in 1 Samuel 16:6-7, "When they had come, he looked at Eliab, and said, 'Surely Yahweh's anointed is before him.' But Yahweh said to Samuel, 'Don't look on his face, or on the height of his stature, because I have rejected him; for I don't see as man sees. For man looks at the outward appearance, but Yahweh looks at the heart.'" We can appear on the outside to be anything we choose. We can present ourselves to the world in certain ways, but God knows who we really are. God sees our heart, and He knows what our true intentions are. We cannot hide our innermost selves from Him.

Perhaps the thought of that is somewhat scary to you. Maybe you are worried about what God is seeing when He examines your heart. I think it is right to be concerned that He can see our hearts. Rather than scare us, however, it should spur us into action. We should pray that the Holy Spirit drives all of the impure motives out of our hearts, so there is no part of us that we are ashamed of, or want to hide. We should pray that He fills our hearts with the love, courage, strength, and ability to do whatever God calls us to do. We should invest in the spiritual disciplines, and pay attention to the examples the Bible gives us of what God looks for in His servants. I find it very reassuring to know that all of these well-known figures mentioned in the Bible had their own failures and flaws, but yet were still loved by Yahweh, and called to serve Him. They had done some wicked things, but if God could heal them and prepare them for service, then I also have a chance.

You may wonder why God would ever choose you to serve Him, when there are clearly better, more obvious choices out there. This is how I felt when He told me I was going to write these books. In my mind, this did not make much sense. I had never written a book before, and I was relatively new to the faith. There are so many famous Christian influencers, Bible experts, or pastors who have written books. I have no following, no audience. The market is flooded with Christian books and materials. My credentials couldn't possibly stack up. I also did not think I had it in me to write one book, let alone five. Writing one was difficult enough. When I have had a long day, I do not feel like writing or editing. I waste time playing mindless games. Surely there is nothing that makes me special, no reason for God to choose me, of all people, to write these books. Someone better is definitely out there.

Then I remembered learning that God does not always have a whole lot of choice when it comes to finding dedicated servants. As stated in Psalm 53:2-3, "God looks down from heaven on the children of men, to see if there are any who understood, who seek after God. Every one of them has gone back. They have become filthy together. There is no one who does good, no, not one." He was looking for someone, anyone, to help share His message with the people, but could not find one person who was seeking to know Him. I may not be the best person the world has to offer, but I am humbly dedicated to serving the Lord. He asked me to write these specific books for specific reasons. While His reasons are usually not understood until later, I do have some guesses. I'm sure much of it has to do with facing my own tests and trials of faith, but the main motivation must be to help share the joy and truth of knowing God.

There may be thousands of books and authors, but many of them were not written with the Holy Spirit, and many even contain false or misleading information. In addition, there are likely thousands of better books on these topics, but my books have been given to people who might otherwise never pick up a Bible, or religious book by any other author. Some people are only reading these books, and thus learning about the Gospel, because of their relationship with me, or someone in my family. These books might never become national best-sellers, but if they change the mind of one non-believer, or help bolster one person's faith, then they have been worth the time, money, and energy needed to produce them. They are one way God has allowed me to share the News with others. They are an in-depth conversation I can have with people, even those whom I may never meet.

God may be asking you to play a particular role simply because you are the only one who can reach a certain person or people. All He needs us to do, is to be obedient to Him when He tells us to do something, and not allow our sense of inadequacy to stop us from following through. You can trust that God has set you up with exactly the background, training, and experience you need for this moment. If the Lord asks you to do something, He will make your efforts successful, no matter how weak, unable, or unqualified you appear to be. Even if that success means you simply bring one other person with you to Christ.

The difficulty of finding faithful humans who will be obedient to Yahweh is lamented in Jeremiah 8:5-8:

> "Why then have the people of Jerusalem fallen back by a perpetual backsliding? They cling to deceit. They refuse to return. I listened and heard, but they didn't say what is right. No one repents of his wickedness, saying, "What have I done?" Everyone turns to his course, as a horse that rushes headlong in the battle. Yes, the stork in the sky knows her appointed times. The turtledove, the swallow, and the crane observe the time of their coming; but my people don't know Yahweh's law. "'How

> do you say, "We are wise, and Yahweh's law is with us"? But, behold, the false pen of the scribes has made that a lie."

The animals know and obey God's voice, but humans have become deaf to the truth of God's Word. We do not even realize we are being disobedient. We go about our daily lives, continually in sin, barely giving God a second thought, but then still claim to know Him and have a relationship with Him. As discussed in the other books in this series, many people who profess to follow Christ have never actually read the Bible for themselves. They trust other people to spoon feed the information to them, and are never taught to invite the Holy Spirit. Without the Holy Spirit, we will struggle to be obedient to God. We will struggle to understand His Word, and we will constantly wrestle with our sins, alone, without the Helper. God has always had to search to find people who were willing to do as Christ said - give up everything, including our lives, to follow Him.

It is not easy to find people who are willing to give up everything they know, and turn their lives over to Him. Sometimes He chooses us because He has no other choice. God uses imperfect people, because imperfect people are the only kind of people who exist. As we have learned, no one is perfect but God. We all just fumble our way through, and we all make a lot of mistakes. We have all sinned. It would be impossible to find just one perfect, sinless person to send out into the world to serve the Lord, let alone millions.

We might find it tempting to judge the people God chooses. When you read the Bible, look at it from the perspective of the people. Remember that they were also human, and would have had strong emotional reactions to the various situations they found themselves in. They also made a lot of mistakes. Sometimes their behaviors seem strange because they were dictated by the customs and morals of the society and time period they lived in. Other times, their experiences can seem relatively universal. When we take the time to put ourselves into their shoes, we can find ourselves learning some valuable lessons about the problems and circumstances in our own lives.

For example, if we start by taking a look at the people Jesus Christ chose to walk with during His time on Earth, we notice that they were not those whom we might expect God to choose. I can't help but think of those scenes in some movies where they put together a top-notch team of people to accomplish a heist or secret rescue mission. They seek out specific people with the unique skills needed to complete the objective, but their choices often look strange from the outside. They may be old and considered past their prime, or an out of shape alcoholic, or cleaned up and married with children, but they are chosen by the ringleader to form the perfect band of misfits.

This is an apt analogy for how it seems Jesus called people to Him. He did not go for the obvious choices: rabbis, Pharisees, or Sadducees. He did not choose someone in the Sanhedrin. He did not choose those who were known for their faith. He did not assemble a wealthy board of directors. He chose poor fishermen, He chose wealthier fishermen, He chose tradespeople, He chose a political rebel, and He even chose a Jewish man who worked as a tax collector for the Romans. These tax collectors were seen as traitors to the Jewish people, and they were reviled.

If we simply look at their outward appearances, His choices made little sense. These were not generally men of great power and influence, either politically, religiously or financially. But Jesus knew their heart, and He knew the tasks He was calling them to do. He knew who He had to call to accomplish His mission. As we have discussed, God also uses weakness to glorify His strength and power. When someone strong and mighty wins a battle, it is expected. When a 'nobody' suddenly has the ear of a king, however, people start to believe God might be involved.

When selecting someone to perform any job, ideally you look for someone who, at a bare minimum, is available to work the hours needed. When you are called by Him, you have to be willing to drop absolutely everything else and go. We see how the first disciples set the example in Matthew 4:18-22:

> Walking by the sea of Galilee, he saw two brothers: Simon, who is called Peter, and Andrew, his brother, casting a net into the sea; for they were fishermen. He said to them, "Come after me, and I will make you fishers for men." They immediately left their nets and followed him. Going on from there, he saw two other brothers, James the son of Zebedee, and John his brother, in the boat with Zebedee their father, mending

> their nets. He called them. They immediately left the boat and their father, and followed him.

When called, they each immediately left their jobs and families behind to follow Jesus. They were literally at work, and walked off the job to follow Him. Are you *that* available to be called by Christ? God looks for people who have faith, and who are available to serve Him. If your friend offered you free tickets for a vacation, but you refused to take the time off of work, she would have to take someone else. If you aren't willing to sacrifice your time to serve and honor Him, then He is unable to choose you.

Now let's put ourselves in their shoes. Imagine you are at work tomorrow, minding your own business. Exhausted, you clean up after a long day, ready to go home, stressed about chores, bills, and kids. You just want to relax and unwind. Then a strange man walks in, and starts preaching and teaching about God while you are finishing up. He calls to you and asks you to do something for Him, or He asks you to drop everything and follow him, right away. Do you do it? Most likely, you will be polite, but tell him that you are closing, and he has to leave. Some people might even threaten to kick him out, or call the police.

What would have to happen for you to do as the disciples did? What must have they each felt or heard to make them immediately listen and obey? Imagine if, like the disciples, you are asked to leave your family and friends behind. Imagine that you have to give up your only source of income, and travel with Him. Now imagine that, because of your wealth and former choice of profession, you are also despised by the rest of the people who are on the team.

Would you have been willing to do it? What if He calls you to do it now? The disciples got to see Jesus in the flesh, but otherwise they did not appear to have had any special knowledge. They were just as likely to misunderstand and make mistakes as we are, even though they could ask Him questions directly. We can still ask Him our questions, by having a relationship with Him through the Holy Spirit. Although they saw Jesus perform miracles, they were often confused, and doubted what they were witnessing. Following Christ required faith then, and it requires faith now. They were not superheroes. They were ordinary people, living ordinary lives, until they were chosen by Christ to abandon those lives, and follow Him. They were just like you and me.

Many other people wanted to be disciples, but when Jesus asked them to follow Him, they made excuses, as we see in Matthew 8:19-22:

> A scribe came and said to him, "Teacher, I will follow you wherever you go." Jesus said to him, "The foxes have holes and the birds of the sky have nests, but the Son of Man has nowhere to lay his head." Another of his disciples said to him, "Lord, allow me first to go and bury my father." But Jesus said to him, "Follow me, and leave the dead to bury their own dead."

This statement might sound harsh to you. It did to me at first. I have heard pastors explain away this statement by saying that the father was not actually dead, and that the man wanted to wait until he died, and was buried, before he followed Jesus.

That may or may not be true, but even if it isn't, it makes no difference.

Jesus was telling them, and us, that when He invites us, we have to go. He was also warning them that a life spent following in His footsteps would not be easy. We have no way of knowing when our 'time' will come, so we have to be prepared. Most people do not understand that when God calls, we have to obey immediately. We cannot hem and haw, or wait until a more convenient time to serve the Lord. We must be available when He calls us. He knows best. All of the cares and concerns that hold us back are only relevant if we do not expect to have eternal life. We know there is a resurrection, and that spreading the Word is the only way to wake people up so their lives can be saved. Therefore, what we have in this life is not what is important. This includes burying our loved ones. All of the other things we cling to instead of God, are merely distractions from doing what He is calling us to do.

As discussed in the other books, God is meant to be our first and foremost priority. Serving Him is not supposed to be an afterthought, or something we do on Sundays for an hour or two after church. Sometimes He calls people to give away money, cars, clothes, houses. Sometimes He calls people to move to another state or country to start a mission or church. Sometimes He calls people to start street preaching, or to evangelize in the workplace. Sometimes He may even just ask you to serve others in some way, or do a job that seems 'beneath' you. You have to be willing to serve however, and whenever, He asks. If you are too busy, you may miss His call for you. It would be highly unusual to apply for a job that starts immediately, but then tell them that you cannot start work until your young children grow up and graduate from high school.

Sometimes this means you will have to make difficult choices, if you intend to follow Christ. If your family and friends are disrupting your ability to focus on, and serve God, you need to make a decision. Whose opinions are more important? Many times, God will ask people to do something that those closest to them cannot understand. They may try to talk you out of doing what you have been asked to do, or belittle you for changing who you are, always focusing on Jesus instead of partying with them. They might get annoyed every time you mention the Bible, or change the station when you are listening to praise and worship music. They might refuse to go to church with you, or to pray together. Will you do it anyway?

Jesus had to set off on His own, despite the concerns, and often disbelief, of his family, and the people he grew up with. In John 6:42, we read of them questioning His claims, "They said, "Isn't this Jesus, the son of Joseph, whose father and mother we know? How then does he say, 'I have come down out of heaven'?" He also faced having to choose His priorities:

> While he was yet speaking to the multitudes, behold, his mother and his brothers stood outside, seeking to speak to him. One said to him, "Behold, your mother and your brothers stand outside, seeking to speak to you. "But he answered him who spoke to him, "Who is my mother? Who are my brothers?" He stretched out his hand toward his disciples, and said, "Behold, my mother and my brothers! For whoever does the will of

> my Father who is in heaven, he is my brother, and sister, and mother." (Matthew 12:46-50)

No one and nothing should stand in the way of your relationship with our Father, so you may have to face some difficult situations. Pray for bravery and strength to stand up and do what is right, even when those you love most don't yet understand and believe what you do. Go to church on your own, watch sermons on your lunch break, pray over those who get in your way, that they may see and learn what you know. Will you still follow Him, even if you are the only one left in the world who does?

The point is, we do not know what God will ask us to do to serve Him, but He is looking for people who are ready and willing to come when He calls them. If you are working 70 hours a week, commuting, and then coming home to obligations with family and friends, how much time are you physically able to devote to the Lord? Do you have people or things in your life that are holding you back from obeying God? You have to free up space in your life to be able to serve Him. The disciples had to be willing to give up everything to follow Jesus. Pray and ask Him to show you any areas of your life that are keeping you from following Him completely.

Are you ready to serve God, and not receive any honor, praise, or glory for the work you do? God searches for those who understand that they are weak without Him, and who are willing to give Him all the honor and glory. Most of the things we are asked to do are not monumental tasks, like building His temple, or the ark. They are more likely to involve one-to-one discipleship. You should not seek to become a famous 'hero of the faith', but rather a fellow servant of the Lord. Among servants, we must remember that we are equals, and should all be working together to serve our King, not trying to achieve glory for ourselves. As the disciples learned, serving God is not about being the best, or most well-known servant:

> He came to Capernaum, and when he was in the house he asked them, "What were you arguing among yourselves on the way?" But they were silent, for they had disputed with one another on the way about who was the greatest. He sat down and called the twelve; and he said to them, "If any man wants to be first, he shall be last of all, and servant of all." (Mark 9:33-35)

It is not a competition because it is not about us. The objective isn't obtaining money, power, and fame for ourselves, it is to bring as many people as possible to repent and return to God. We are nothing without God, so whenever we accomplish any task, big or small, all glory, honor and credit must be given to Him. We have been told of the coming reward of eternal life without evil, so we do not need to worry about temporary rewards here and now. Pray and ask for help to let go of your ego and pride. Remember where your help comes from.

In *Pursuit to Commitment*, we spent a chapter learning about how our trials and training prepare us for resisting the enemy's temptations. They also prepare us to serve the Lord. God looks for people who are faithful and committed, whether times are good or bad. He needs people who are willing to endure until the end, keeping their faith, and obeying Him. Following Christ is not an easy path. It was not easy for Him, it was not easy for the disciples, it has never been easy for any figure mentioned in the Bible, and it will not be easy for us either.

We know the enemy will continue to fire attacks our way, even though we are safe now on God's side. We discussed how to repel those attacks, and resist the temptations to return to your old way of life. We do this by standing on the stronghold of God's promises, through practicing the spiritual disciplines. You will need this solid foundation as you complete the work you are given. You cannot dabble, you have to study and learn, and be trained in being a disciple of God. If you do not focus on your training for the battle, you will end up nowhere, and lost. This is a life and death battle for your soul, and the souls of those you love and care about, it is the most important thing you will ever do. It is worth your time and effort.

Are you faithful in these disciplines, with a heart that yearns to know and learn from God? The Lord is not looking for those who already feel like they know how to do everything, He is looking for those who are trainable, and ready to submit to His coaching. The initial goal is to get it through our heads that we need the help of God, so we will ask for it. The next goal is to remind us that we get our help from Him, so we will always seek Him as our first resort. As stated in Psalms 121:1-2, He is our only source of help, "I will lift up my eyes to the hills. Where does my help come from? My help comes from Yahweh, who made heaven and earth." Our job is to learn how to live righteously, always seeking growth by calling upon Him to help us. If we are not already obedient to Him in the everyday, little things, such as prayer and studying scripture, how could we possibly be ready to handle a much more daunting task? If we are not seeking His help, and learning to hear His voice now, how will we know how to communicate with Him when things get more difficult?

It is imperative to realize that part of being ready to be called includes all of that coaching and preparation. He needs you to get to know Him, and learn how to trust Him, before He sends you out into the world. He spends time preparing you, through the processes discussed in *Pursuit to Commitment*. This means that, from now on, throughout your entire life, you are still actively involved in your ongoing sanctification process. You have to seek freedom from sin. You do not have to already be sinless and perfect, but you do have to be free from giving your life to sin. To be usable by God, you must become a vessel that is sanctified and neat. You must be willing to be purged, cleansed, and purified.

You have to be filled with His light from the inside, in order to project it to the outside. What you focus on, what you look at, determines what you are filled with. Do you keep your eye on the Lord? Always seeking to know Him and His will? Or do you focus on seeking the things you wish you could have in this world? Do you focus on what you do not have? Do you focus on the pleasures you want to obtain? Do you focus on all of the pains and problems you are subjected to? As Jesus said in Matthew 6:22-23, "The lamp of the body is the eye. If therefore your eye is sound, your whole body will be full of light. But if your eye is evil, your whole body will be full of darkness. If therefore the light that is in you is darkness, how great is the darkness!"

Our eyes. If we think about it, they truly are the lamps of our bodies. They project much of what we feel to the outside world (eye rolls, soul gazing stares, shifting or hiding our eyes when we lie). They also project much of the outside world to our brain. If we focus on our problems, and the negativity of the world, we will see so much darkness around us. If, however, we have chosen to follow the Lord, then we must seek to see only Him.

God is light and love, so if we seek Him, and Him alone, our eyes will only see light and love. If light and love is all we can see, then the only thing we will think about is light and love. When we are filled with light and God's love, then our eyes are projecting that light and love to everyone around us. We will give off love and positivity, and project God's mercy to others. We will also see others more closely to how He sees them, simply hurting humans, tempted by the evil forces in this world. They are in need of finding the oil of the Holy Spirit to light their own lamps. If you are filled with God's light, you will be able to teach and help others to be filled with His light. On the other hand, if we do not choose to keep our eyes on Him, then our only other option is to look at, focus on, and see, darkness and evil.

Er...stop, am I really saying that if we do not follow God, we are following evil? Yes. That is exactly what I am saying, because that is exactly what the Bible says. Those are our only two options. Darkness or Light. If we turn away from the light, all that is left is darkness. As Jesus told us in Matthew 12:30, "He who is not with me is against me, and he who doesn't gather with me, scatters." Every single time we drop our focus from God, we start to falter and stray from the light. This reminds me of Peter, when Jesus called him out of the boat in Matthew 14. Peter stepped off the boat in the middle of the sea and walked on the water, toward Jesus. As long as Peter kept his focus on Jesus, he did not even notice the wind, or the darkness of the sea all around him, and he stayed above the water. As soon as he turned his eyes away from Jesus, he saw the darkness and the waves. It scared him, then he began to sink. The only thing that saved him was calling upon Jesus, who pulled him out of trouble.

In Joel 2:32 we read, "It will happen that whoever will call on Yahweh's name shall be saved", and the scripture is repeated again in Romans 10, but then in Matthew 7:21-27, Jesus says:

> Not everyone who says to me, 'Lord, Lord,' will enter into the Kingdom of Heaven, but he who does the will of my Father who is in heaven. Many will tell me in that day, 'Lord, Lord, didn't we prophesy in your name, in your name cast out demons, and in your name do many mighty works?' Then I will tell them, 'I never knew you. Depart from me, you who work iniquity.' Everyone therefore who hears these words of mine and does them, I will liken him to a wise man who built his house on a rock. The rain came down, the floods came, and the winds blew and beat on that house; and it didn't fall, for it was founded on the rock. Everyone who hears these words of mine and doesn't do them will be like a

> foolish man who built his house on the sand. The rain came down, the floods came, and the winds blew and beat on that house; and it fell—and its fall was great."

What is the deal? Why is there this contradiction? If we call on His name are we saved or not?

To resolve it, we have to distinguish between being saved, and entering the Kingdom. Through the sacrifice of Jesus, we have all been offered eternal life. As we read in Revelation 5:9, in part, our souls were bought at the cost of the sacrifice of Jesus, "Worthy are You to take the scroll and to break its seals; for You were slaughtered, and You purchased *people* for God with Your blood from every tribe, language, people, and nation." He purchased us from death for God, but in the end we will be called up, and must be judged:

> But when the Son of Man comes in his glory, and all the holy angels with him, then he will sit on the throne of his glory. Before him all the nations will be gathered, and he will separate them one from another, as a shepherd separates the sheep from the goats. He will set the sheep on his right hand, but the goats on the left. Then the King will tell those on his right hand, 'Come, blessed of my Father, inherit the Kingdom prepared for you from the foundation of the world; for I was hungry and you gave me food to eat. I was thirsty and you gave me drink. I was a stranger and you took me in. I was naked and you clothed me. I was sick and you visited me. I was in prison and you came to me.' "Then the righteous will answer him, saying, 'Lord, when did we see you hungry and feed you, or thirsty and give you a drink? When did we see you as a stranger and take you in, or naked and clothe you? When did we see you sick or in prison and come to you?' "The King will

> answer them, 'Most certainly I tell you, because you did it to one of the least of these my brothers, you did it to me.' Then he will say also to those on the left hand, 'Depart from me, you cursed, into the eternal fire which is prepared for the devil and his angels; for I was hungry, and you didn't give me food to eat; I was thirsty, and you gave me no drink; I was a stranger, and you didn't take me in; naked, and you didn't clothe me; sick, and in prison, and you didn't visit me.' "Then they will also answer, saying, 'Lord, when did we see you hungry, or thirsty, or a stranger, or naked, or sick, or in prison, and didn't help you?' "Then he will answer them, saying, 'Most certainly I tell you, because you didn't do it to one of the least of these, you didn't do it to me.' These will go away into eternal punishment, but the righteous into eternal life. (Matthew 25:31-46)

We will be held accountable for our sins. If we have submitted to God, and have built a relationship with the Lord, we will have been purged of our evil, and allowed to enter the Kingdom. Many people claim that they believe, but there is no evidence that their hearts have changed. There are no fruits of the Spirit. As many have pointed out, even the devil believes in God. Believing in Him is different from following Him. There is also a distinction between a believer crying out, and calling on His name, and imposters who use His name as a means of self-glorification. They give lip service to God, and seek to show off great works of prophecy and demon-casting, but are not interested in the humble servitude that comes with following and knowing Christ. Jesus is making a distinction between hypocrites who invoke God to control others, or to make a name for themselves, versus true believers who cry out to, and yearn for Him with all their heart and soul.

You cannot claim Christ in name only. You cannot live your life as you see fit, and then only call on the Lord when it suits you. You cannot claim fidelity to Yahweh, but then also still be caught up in the worship of idols, such as money, popularity, or superstition. If you truly believe that Yahweh is real, and you will have eternal life with Him, you must allow Him to transform you. You must believe and be faithful enough to actually change your life to follow Him. Have you formed your own relationship with Christ? Do you talk to God? Do you obey? Are you just doing things here and there, pretending to be Christian, but doing them without love, or to bolster your own pride? Do you continue to sin without the conviction and correction of the Holy Spirit?

He may also work to build up your level of obedience. He checks to see if you are listening for, and in tune with, His voice, and if you are willing to do whatever little task He whispers to you. He will give you the responsibility you prove yourself capable of handling. If He repeatedly gives you the nudge to go talk to someone, and you repeatedly ignore Him, why would He trust you with a bigger task, such as speaking to a church full of people? If you do not help the less fortunate with your time, money, or resources now, why would He give you more? This is the concept Jesus explained to us in the parable of the talents, found in Matthew 25:14-30:

> "For it is like a man going into another country, who called his own servants and entrusted his goods to them. To one he gave five talents, to another two, to

another one, to each according to his own ability. Then he went on his journey. Immediately he who received the five talents went and traded with them, and made another five talents. In the same way, he also who got the two gained another two. But he who received the one talent went away and dug in the earth and hid his lord's money. "Now after a long time the lord of those servants came, and settled accounts with them. He who received the five talents came and brought another five talents, saying, 'Lord, you delivered to me five talents. Behold, I have gained another five talents in addition to them.' "His lord said to him, 'Well done, good and faithful servant. You have been faithful over a few things, I will set you over many things. Enter into the joy of your lord.' "He also who got the two talents came and said, 'Lord, you delivered to me two talents. Behold, I have gained another two talents in addition to them.' "His lord said to him, 'Well done, good and faithful servant. You have been faithful over a few things. I will set you over many things. Enter into the joy of your lord.' "He also who had received the one talent came and said, 'Lord, I knew you that you are a hard man, reaping where you didn't sow, and gathering where you didn't scatter. I was afraid, and went away and hid your talent in the earth. Behold, you have what is yours.' But his lord answered him, 'You wicked and slothful servant. You knew that I reap where I didn't sow, and gather where I didn't scatter. You ought therefore to have deposited my money with the bankers, and at my coming I should have received back my own with interest. Take away therefore the talent from him and give it to him who has the ten talents. For to everyone who has will be given, and he will have abundance, but from him who doesn't have, even that which he has will be taken away. Throw out the unprofitable servant into

> the outer darkness, where there will be weeping and gnashing of teeth.'

Talents represented a very large amount of money that was entrusted to each servant. When we consider the parable in terms of our obedience, we see that we have to use what He gives us, what we currently have, and be obedient with it. We must use the talents He has given us, in ways that help grow the Lord's kingdom.

Jesus is urging us to increase our talents, by increasing the number of brothers and sisters who believe. If we encourage people, who then become believers, and they also surrender and become obedient to Him, then His kingdom has just grown. Jesus said the disciples should be fishers of men, and that the harvest is ripe. People are the prize. God sees our souls, the souls of His children, as the most valuable thing, so every soul we save increases the value of His kingdom. In turn, each believer is called to the Great Commission (which we will cover in Chapter 4). By telling others about Christ, and helping them seek Him, we can double or triple our own 'talents'.

Once we become servants of God, He entrusts us with a talent - His most priceless possessions - other humans. We should be investing ourselves into increasing our talents, by lovingly showing our brothers and sisters the way to the foot of the cross. God has already given us each the unique ability to break through the resistance of certain people, and to encourage them to exercise their free will by choosing Yahweh over Satan. If we hide our talent away, and never tell anyone about God, then we have wasted His plan for us, and left our brothers and sisters in danger. Pray for the ability to bring as many people as possible with you!

If you want to be chosen by God, it also doesn't hurt if you request an assignment. Ask Him to choose you. As I shared in *Pursuit to Commitment*, when I asked God to send me, it became a full soul-searching. A test of my willingness to give everything up to Him, myself and my whole life as a living sacrifice. It can be scary to ask Him to choose you, because you don't know what He might ask, and because you have to commit without knowing how it will all work out. Submitting to sanctification is a difficult process. Allowing the Holy Spirit to search your soul, taking an inventory of every secret thing you think only you know about, is intimidating, terrifying, guilt-inducing, painful, confusing, and honestly just about every emotion wrapped into one.

But it is worth it. It feels so freeing each time I feel Him dig another poisonous root of bitterness and shame out of my soul. Getting to know God is an absolutely amazing, awesome experience. Living for eternity in perfect peace, joy, and love, is worth whatever it takes. Allow Him to take full control, helping guide your every decision. Stay attuned to His voice, following His lead. He will cleanse you and prepare you for the job He wants you to do. Then you will be ready to accept the job you asked for.

When He calls you to do something, remember that there is always a specific reason He chose you. As Mordecai told Esther, "Who knows if you haven't come to the kingdom for such a time as this?" (Esther 4:14, in part). God had placed

Esther in her position as the queen, specifically so that she would have the opportunity to save the Jews. The same reasoning applies to the tasks God asks you to do. If, through prayer, and practice in the spiritual disciplines, you have been given direction from God to do something, you should confidently follow through with it. After all, it could be, while you may not understand the full scope of His plan now, He has placed you in a particular city, job, or circumstance for a very specific purpose. Your job might give you unique access to certain people who can help the cause. You might be the one person who knows exactly the right things to say to convince one particularly stubborn atheist that God is real, and Christ died for our sins. You might be the archeologist who discovers some key biblical artifact, the existence of which convinces thousands of people to turn to Christ. Anything is possible when God is involved!

Don't put your own expectations on what God will ask of you. Just obey. Some people assume that a calling from God has to be something magnificent, like being a mega-church pastor, or that you will have to do something drastic, like move to another country to be a missionary. In reality, the world may never know your name, and you might be asked to serve right where you are, but rest assured that God knows you. Do not worry about how spectacular or difficult the assignment is. Just complete it.

Once Esther had completed her assignment, there was no mention of any other things she had to do. Do not discount what God calls you to do, because of some preconceived notion you have about what such a calling should look like. Throw out any ideas you have about how risky, grand, or involved your job should be, or how long your assignment should last. Just listen and try to obey. Perhaps you were also created 'for such a time as this' and now is your one shot, your one chance to get this right, by obeying whatever God tells you to do.

There are infinite ways God can use your particular skill, talent, location, position, influence, or power. The goal is to stay constantly tuned into listening for His voice, and to be dedicated to walking in obedience daily like Christ was. When God calls you to your assignment, it may look very different from someone else's calling. God has the perfect plan for each of us, to bring us to Him. When we do return, He has the perfect plan for each of us to invite our brothers and sisters to come home too. Because we, as individuals, have unique ideas, interests, and beliefs, we each require different things to help us wake up, and open our minds to the Lord. He uses our unique experiences to serve the exact purposes He has planned. As you read, think of ways you can be more available and obedient to Yahweh, and how you can focus on Him more diligently.

Eventually we need to get to a place within ourselves where we are fully available to do His bidding. We have to be completely, fully submitted, ready to go wherever He sends us, or to do whatever He tells us to do, at the drop of a hat. We have to learn how to stop arguing and negotiating with Him. We have to stop trying to do things our way instead of His. We have to pay attention to His lessons, and seek out His instruction. We have to be willing to humble ourselves, and do any job He gives us, without worrying about how enjoyable the job is, or our own reward. We will not always be able to understand God's will, or His reasons for asking us to do something. Therefore, we have to be willing to have faith, and commit to His will, even when we do not fully understand what it is, or why we were given a certain task. We have to learn to trust in Him completely.

Notes

3

Be the Church

But be doers of the word, and not only hearers, deluding your own selves. For if anyone is a hearer of the word and not a doer, he is like a man looking at his natural face in a mirror; for he sees himself, and goes away, and immediately forgets what kind of man he was. But he who looks into the perfect law of freedom and continues, not being a hearer who forgets but a doer of the work, this man will be blessed in what he does.

- James 1:22-25

Some churches welcome everyone, some only certain people, and some require membership. Some are stoic and serious, some dance and sing. Some are rigid and condemning, some are open and forgiving. Some are high on ceremony and formality, others teach in jeans and T-shirts. How do we know what the church should be? Of course you know my answer: pray about it, and read the Bible. To me, the obvious place to start seemed to be figuring out what is expected or appropriate for those calling themselves Christians, and their churches. According to Jesus, there are certain things believers, and unbelievers, should expect to see from churches and their members. Unfortunately, far too often what Jesus taught, is not what happens in practice.

When we decide to follow Christ, we become 'the church'. Most of us need some initial time in a church to help us learn and understand what we read. At some point, once we understand the Bible, and submit to God, we have to go from sitting and getting *from* the church, to helping and doing *as* the church. The church is not meant to be the building. It should be a group of believers, who form a family of brothers and sisters. The entire family should be united to support one another in the mission of adding more people to the family. We do this by spreading God's message to unbelievers, and supporting our fellow believers in their faith, each of us serving in roles best suited to our strengths.

In fact, in many parts of the world, believers are unable to gather at a large building to publicly teach and worship together. When we think about it, these courageous people are blessed in a way that we are not. They cannot rely on a building, so they are forced to actively 'be the church'. Our buildings must simply serve as a place for the church to meet, and meeting together is important. What is more important, is that the building does not become a way for the church to be closed off and secretive.

Ensure church buildings are not hiding places, for members to become insulated and separated from society. Ensure they are not hang-out spots, for everyone to become complacent, and lazy, repeating the same messages to the same group of people, week after week, and year after year. Ensure they are not judgmental and exclusionary, keeping out the people who do not look the part. If our churches are instead welcoming, truthful, and Spirit-filled, the building can serve as a great place to bring new people to hear the Word. The more seasoned members should love, serve, and rejoice in every single person who walks in the door. We should be honored that God has given us the opportunity to teach them about our salvation.

As believers who form the church, we must become a beacon of God's love to the world. Jesus compares His followers to the natural elements of salt and light:

> You are the salt of the earth, but if the salt has lost its flavor, with what will it be salted? It is then good for nothing, but to be cast out and trodden under the feet of men. You are the light of the world. A city located on a hill can't be hidden. Neither do you light a lamp and put it under a measuring basket, but on a stand; and it shines to all who are in the house. Even so, let your light shine before men, that they may see your good works

> and glorify your Father who is in heaven. (Matthew 5:13-16)

People, both well-meaning and ill-intentioned, may argue that this statement is slightly problematic. After all, unadulterated pure salt is a mineral, and cannot lose its flavor. But that is exactly the point. Salt cannot lose its flavor, so salt is always good for something, and should not be trodden underfoot. There is nothing else exactly like salt; nothing could restore salt if it ever lost its saltiness. This is also an admonition to us that we should not give up our saltiness and light, by allowing ourselves to be trampled into the mud, or hidden under a shade. This happens when we turn back to the world, and away from God.

The very next line says you are a city on a hill, the light of the world, you cannot be hidden. You can see a city on a hill from miles away. Then he gives another example, no one would light a lamp, only to put it under a basket so no one could see the light. Oil was far too expensive to waste lighting the inside of a basket. Wars have been fought over salt. Once you awaken and realize who you are, and to Whom you belong, you become salt, you become the light. You cannot lose your flavor, and you must reflect His light to the world.

Far from hidden, or worthy of being trodden underfoot, you are sought after, valuable, and important. To us, salt and light may seem cheap and common. We merely buy salt at the store, or flick a switch to turn on the lights. Of course, they were not always so easy to obtain. Throughout history, they have always been highly prized, as they serve many important functions. I remember an old fable I heard as a child that spoke to me, as I have always loved extra salt on my food. The author is unknown, and there are many versions in many cultures, but I remember it went something like this:

A king had three daughters and he asked them to show him how much they loved him. He was pleased with the lavish demonstrations of the two older sisters, but he threw his youngest daughter out of his kingdom when she simply told him she loved him as much as she loved salt in her food. He found her statement insulting. Where was the big show? How could she only love her father as much as she loved common table salt? After being cast out, she eventually found work as a cook, and moved her way up, until one day, she catered an event at the palace. She ensured that no salt was put into any of the dishes. When the king demanded to know why the food was so awful and tasteless, she told him how she had left out the salt. This made him realize how essential salt was to the flavor of the meal. She revealed who she was, and he quickly understood that by comparing her love for her father to salt, she was demonstrating how essential he was to her life. Of course, upon recognizing her, and realizing how much she loved him, he wept and apologized.

Salt and light act in so many ways that we can metaphorically apply to our lives. For example, salt in the above story was a flavor enhancer, bringing out herbs and spices, and adding life and zest to each dish. The meal was 'loveless' and 'lifeless' without the salt. Light also works in a similar fashion. Our eyes cannot perceive color without light.

Sit in a windowless room and observe the colors you can see. Then turn off the light and look around. The colors disappear. All life and zest leave the room, and you are left with a bland assortment of grays.

In the same way, one of our jobs is to bring out the flavor, and add our life and zest to God's Word. We become the salt and light, enhancing and illuminating God's Word, when we share our own personal testimony with others. When we talk about our own struggle with recovery, or the empowerment God gave us to leave a bad situation, we add a relatable face to accompany the biblical lessons, and bring them to life. It is why different people prefer different pastors and teachers. We all have different learning styles and communication preferences that affect our ability to understand a message. Hearing the Bible discussed by people who share similar experiences to ours, can help it 'taste better' or help us 'see the light'.

Salt and light share another quality with believers, in that they both spread out to reach further. If I add salt to a pot of boiling water, it does not just make some of the water salty. It dissolves, making the entire pot of water taste salty. If I turn on a lamp, the light does not stay in one spot, it fills the room. When I toured the Mammoth caves in Kentucky, we experienced absolute darkness. We were deep enough underground that no natural light could reach us, sitting in a huge open auditorium. Everyone was instructed to put away watches, or any other items that could give off any light (we did not have phones like we do now). Then they turned off the lights, and you could not see anything. The darkness was so complete your eyes would never adjust.

Suddenly, the tour guide lit a single tiny match, and the entire cavernous space was instantly filled with light. In the same way, we are called to spread out and fill the Earth with God's love, and the message of our salvation. We must spread like salt and light into the world, sharing freely with everyone. We must permeate the world with His Word, making everyone salty, and reflecting the light of God to all.

Salt is necessary for life. It also preserves and protects. We cure meats in salt, and pack food in salt to preserve it. Our job is to preserve the Word of God on the Earth, by telling others about Him, and writing His words on our hearts. We must protect our loved ones by helping them understand, and encouraging them to follow Christ. Salt cleanses and heals. Like when we gargle with salt water for a toothache. When we share the Good News with others, and they invite the Holy Spirit, they can be cleansed and healed. Salt can clear a path, when it is used in colder climates to melt ice and snow in the streets and sidewalks. When we share Jesus, we share the Way, the clear path to eternal life.

Light is also essential to our life. Light is required for us to see clearly. In fact, some of the animals that lived down in the caves in that absolute darkness had no eyes at all, because they were not able to use them. When we share the light of God's Word, we help open the eyes of the blind. Light is necessary for plants to make their food, which they convert into the form of energy we need for our earthly sustenance.

When we share the light of God, we share the Bread of Life, providing us eternal sustenance. Light helps us find our way, our headlights illuminate the road ahead, a night light can help us find the bathroom at 3:00 am, and lighted exit signs and paths in a theater or airplane show us the way out in case of danger. The light of God, when shared with others, guides them out of the darkness. We help reflect His light onto the one true path to salvation.

But too much salt can ruin the flavor of a meal, or at worst, be deadly. When salt overpowers the food it was meant to enhance, it becomes inedible. When we become more glorified than God in our minds, we become too salty, and we overpower His message with our own. We must remember that salt's job is to dissolve, and highlight the other flavors, not become more than the meal itself. In the same way, we must not seek our own glory, but remain in the background, highlighting God, and pointing always to Him, not ourselves.

Too much light can burn us. If our light becomes the focus, we can attempt to stand in the way of God's light, blocking it, and creating a shadow. When we usurp God's light, claiming His glory as our own, we risk being burned by our ambition. We must remember where our light comes from. We can block His light by seeking our own glory. We then force others to stand in the shadow we cast, which prevents them from feeling His light, and learning about His love and mercy. We must make sure the salt and light within us does not overpower, or overshadow, the Source it came from.

We are like salt and light, and can become powerful and beneficial to the world around us. If we surrender fully, and keep the Holy Spirit within us, we cannot lose our saltiness and light. If we focus too much on the world, we can allow the enemy to trample us, and dampen our shine. We are children of God, but the enemy wants to convince us that we have lost our flavor, or the love of God, and therefore we are worthy only of being trodden on. We are meant to be a city on a hill, a lamp that is lit, but the enemy wants to put a basket over the light of God that shines within each of us. He wants to make us forget who we are! We allow ourselves to be trampled and hidden away, when we stop producing fruit. When we stop sharing the Gospel. When we go through the motions, but no longer allow the Holy Spirit to change our life and heart. When we give up. Part of our role as the church is to be like salt and light for others. This means we must retain our saltiness and light until the very end, and not allow ourselves to be trampled or hidden away.

Accomplishing this goal means living God's Word as an example to the world. God's Word is in the Bible. We have talked in the previous books about some of the dangers of clinging to 'religion' over the Bible. I cannot tell you how many comments I have read or heard, from people who claim to be Christian, saying that the Bible is not meant to be taken literally, that many of the events, as described, did not happen. There are even many formal denominations, and some loosely Christian-based cults, that take parts of the Bible literally, but then claim that their church laws, pamphlets, additional books, doctrine, or canon trump the Bible.

One of the main goals of these books is to get people to realize that we are absolutely meant to take the events of the Bible literally, and neither add to, nor take away from, God's Word within it. This is why I encourage everyone to read it for themselves, and I pray the glimpses of the Bible stories shared in these books spark your curiosity to read the entire thing. The New Testament is a completion of the Old Covenant that God made in the Old Testament. It is the final promise to all humanity that everyone who believes in, and calls upon, Christ will be saved and sanctified.

The story is finished, we have been shown the path to salvation. We just have to choose and follow the path, and then share the story with others, so they can make their own choice. There is nothing new to add to what the Bible already tells us, we just have to help each other find out about it. We can each hear direct instruction from Him once we have invited the Holy Spirit to live within us, but the complete details of our salvation are set out already in the Bible. The only thing we bring to the table is our testimony of how He saved us, and sharing how the lessons from the Bible apply to our modern lives. We do not need to invent new rituals, laws, or promises, we need to learn and obey what He has already given us.

Taking the Bible literally does not mean that every single word written within its pages is true, or that every word contained therein is God's Word. Taking it literally simply means believing that the events and conversations happened as they are described, not that everything they said in those conversations is an accurate proclamation about God. Many people try to argue that because “all scripture is God-breathed”, somehow this means that absolutely every statement made within the Bible is correct. Clearly that is not the case. The Bible tells us how people actually were, and they got things wrong a lot. It points out the many mistakes, false idol worship, and false doctrine spread by the people, as a contrast to God’s true Word. There are also several parables that are sort of ‘realistic fiction’ stories, used as metaphors for explaining the complex concepts of the spiritual realm, such as who God is, what Heaven is like, and how to find eternal life.

You cannot simply take a random quote from the Bible and attribute any meaning to it, without knowing what the context was, who said it, why they said it, and what God’s reaction was to it. Job’s friends preached false doctrine to him; if you quoted what Eliphaz or Bildad said as ‘God’s Word’ you would be wrong. Contrast what Jesus says with what the Pharisees, Romans, or even the New Testament authors said. Paul and others even tell us some of their statements come from their own opinions. When this happens, we must compare their statements with what God says, before we accept their personal opinions as truth. It is like I say about these books, do not just take anyone’s word for it, compare everything with God’s Word - after all, His Word is all that matters.

When reading the Bible, you must differentiate between when a human speaks, versus when God speaks. You have to read the Bible as a complete work, and understand how it all fits together. Many rules and covenants were specific to a time and place, or even to specific people. Many worshiped false gods, and committed outrageous acts of evil. Scripture is God-breathed, and useful for instruction, but, as part of that instruction, we should receive a gift of discernment, to be able to determine what is said by Yahweh and Jesus, and what is said by humans. We have to learn how to distinguish between false prophecy, and the true Word of God. Jesus constantly reminds us to be on the lookout for false prophets, wolves in sheep's clothing. We must know scripture well, in order to guard against those who pretend to be followers of Christ, but then sneakily encourage us to do things that violate God's law.

Reading it literally also does not mean that we have to do everything the people in the Bible did. Not everything that applied to biblical figures applies to us. For example, Samson was a Nazarite to God and was given great power, so long as he did not cut his hair. The rest of us do not have that specific deal, so we can cut our hair. His story, and others in the Bible, should serve as examples to us of how easily we are tempted and deceived. Samson's story wasn't about his hair. It shows us what could happen if we take our eyes off God, and become arrogant, thinking that it is our own strength that saves us, instead of a gift given from God. It shows us that we shouldn't be flippant with the gifts He provides, putting our passions and desires above honoring God. It shows us what happens when we trust the wrong people, instead of keeping our trust in Him.

Aside from the basic foundational components of our faith, why don't the same directions apply to everyone? The specific instructions God gives to people are different almost every time. This forces us to stay in constant contact with Him. The only way we know what we are supposed to do, is by focusing on His Word, and His voice, through our own relationship with Him. Following God's Word is not about memorizing a bunch of rituals and rules from the Bible or belonging to a particular church. It is about knowing and understanding His will for all humanity. It is about learning from the examples of the people who came before us, in the hopes that we do not repeat their mistakes.

We must be very careful that we stick to God's Word in the Bible, and speak through the Holy Spirit when teaching others. It is very clear that we should not be adding to, or taking away from His Word:

> Every word of God is flawless. He is a shield to those who take refuge in him. Don't you add to his words, lest he reprove you, and you be found a liar. (Proverbs 30:5-6)

> You shall not add to the word which I command you, neither shall you take away from it, that you may keep the commandments of Yahweh your God which I command you. (Deuteronomy 4:2)

> Will you speak unrighteously for God, and talk deceitfully for him? Will you show partiality to him? Will you contend for God? Is it good that he should search you out? Or as one deceives a man, will you deceive him? He will surely reprove you if you secretly show partiality. Won't his majesty make you afraid and his

> dread fall on you? Your memorable sayings are proverbs of ashes. (Job 13:7-12)
>
> I testify to everyone who hears the words of the prophecy of this book: if anyone adds to them, God will add to him the plagues which are written in this book. If anyone takes away from the words of the book of this prophecy, God will take away his part from the tree of life, and out of the holy city, which are written in this book. He who testifies these things says, "Yes, I am coming soon." Amen! Yes, come, Lord Jesus! (Revelation 22:18-20)

We are to obey only God's Word, not conflicting rules and rituals dictated by random people. This includes all of the people of the Bible. Any person or church who tells you otherwise has now admitted they have deviated from God's Word to making up their own rules. If we do not take the Bible literally, and strive to understand its meaning, then what else could we possibly be basing our beliefs on? By not following God's Word, each church is then creating its own new god from thin air.

Everything a church teaches as doctrine, that is not based in God's Word, must naturally come from their own human imaginations and desires. This is why so many different denominations and cults exist. They loosely follow parts of the Bible, picking and choosing those aspects of God's Word that fit their own agenda, in order to please people, rather than making their agenda align with God's, and pleasing Him. Some add female deities, glorify people, or worship images, for example. When we are filled with the Holy Spirit, we know God's Word, we love God's Word, we cling to it, read it, and ask

Him to cleanse us until we wholeheartedly live it. You know you are in a church where the Word is understood, taught, and lived, when its members are welcoming, knowledgeable, and love to discuss the Bible. You will see it in their words and actions.

We can read the messages given to the main churches established at the time, admonishing them on areas of weakness. By looking at them, we can develop a clearer picture of our role as Christians, and what our role should be as 'the church'. Let's take a look at the instructions Jesus gave, beginning with Ephesus in Revelation 2:2-7:

> I know your works, and your toil and perseverance, and that you can't tolerate evil men, and have tested those who call themselves apostles, and they are not, and found them false. You have perseverance and have endured for my name's sake, and have not grown weary. But I have this against you, that you left your first love. Remember therefore from where you have fallen, and repent and do the first works; or else I am coming to you swiftly, and will move your lamp stand out of its place, unless you repent. But this you have, that you hate the works of the Nicolaitans, which I also hate. He who has an ear, let him hear what the Spirit says to the assemblies. To him who overcomes I will give to eat from the tree of life, which is in the Paradise of my God.

This church had done well at understanding God's Word and testing false prophets, even those who claimed to be apostles. They also opposed the Nicolaitans, who may have been allowing people to continue to participate in their familiar pagan practices, along with worshiping Yahweh, in essence keeping one foot in each world. They knew people cannot serve two masters. We have to pick a side and obey only God. Unfortunately, despite their discernment, they had lost their love and passion for Christ. They used to be excited about knowing God, and worshiped out of their abundance of love. Lately, they had grown weary and lackluster, knowing the truth, but not living it. We must make sure we never allow ourselves to slow down, and become lazy and complacent in our faith, or we will not be prepared when it is tested. We must keep a zeal in our relationship with Him.

Next we move to verses 9-11, the church at Smyrna:

> I know your works, oppression, and your poverty (but you are rich), and the blasphemy of those who say they are Jews, and they are not, but are a synagogue of Satan. Don't be afraid of the things which you are about to suffer. Behold, the devil is about to throw some of you into prison, that you may be tested; and you will have oppression for ten days. Be faithful to death, and I will give you the crown of life. He who has an ear, let him hear what the Spirit says to the assemblies. He who overcomes won't be harmed by the second death.

This church is doing well, poor in material wealth, but rich in spiritual wealth. He warns them that bad times and attacks are coming, but to hold fast to what they know. We learn that we must be faithful and unafraid, even when we are suffering and oppressed. People in many countries are thrown into prison for their belief in God, and tortured to death for their testimony, so we must be prepared that, one day, this could happen to any of us. We have to have a firm foundation in Christ to withstand it. Do not wait until it starts happening to start praying.

To Pergamum, He warns:

> I know your works and where you dwell, where Satan's throne is. You hold firmly to my name, and didn't deny my faith in the days of Antipas my witness, my faithful one, who was killed among you, where Satan dwells. But I have a few things against you, because you have there some who hold the teaching of Balaam, who taught Balak to throw a stumbling block before the children of Israel, to eat things sacrificed to idols, and to commit sexual immorality. So also you likewise have some who hold to the teaching of the Nicolaitans. Repent therefore, or else I am coming to you quickly and I will make war against them with the sword of my mouth. He who has an ear, let him hear what the Spirit says to the assemblies. To him who overcomes, to him I will give of the hidden manna, and I will give him a white stone, and on the stone a new name written which no one knows but he who receives it. (Revelation 2:13-17)

Here, the church is noted for their ability to maintain their faith in the midst of one of the most evil places. Even when Antipas was killed (possibly burned alive inside a copper bull) for spreading the faith, they held firm. However, they are warned that if they do not restore or remove those who stray to other false gods, He will come to judge them.

Balaam was an Old Testament figure who was unable to curse the Israelites in a major battle. He fled, and then since he couldn't curse them, he seems to have worked with the Midianites to try to trick the Isrealites into abandoning Yahweh. He convinced them to be relaxed in their adherence to the laws, and worship the false god, Baal. Note that Jesus cautions them to be wary of those false prophets who encourage eating meat sacrificed to idols, and other idolatrous practices.

When people claim to follow the Bible, but then twist God's Word with their own false practices and doctrine, it causes extreme damage. People will either believe and practice the false teachings, and be subject to judgment, or they will turn away from God, because of the misleading information they have been taught. We must reject the teachings of those who falsely preach and twist His Word. We must also be cautious that we are not inadvertently incorporating false doctrine into our own beliefs.

The church at Thyatira is up next, in Revelation 2:19-27:

> I know your works, your love, faith, service, patient endurance, and that your last works are more than the first. But I have this against you, that you tolerate your woman Jezebel, who calls herself a prophetess. She teaches and seduces my servants to commit sexual immorality and to eat things sacrificed to idols. I gave her time to repent, but she refuses to repent of her sexual immorality. Behold, I will throw her and those who commit adultery with her into a bed of great oppression, unless they repent of her works. I will kill her children with Death, and all the assemblies will know that I am he who searches the minds and hearts. I will give to each one of you according to your deeds. But to you I say, to the rest who are in Thyatira—as many as don't have this teaching, who don't know what some call 'the deep things of Satan'—to you I say, I am not putting any other burden on you. Nevertheless, hold that which you have firmly until I come. He who overcomes, and he who keeps my works to the end, to him I will give authority over the nations. He will rule them with a rod

> of iron, shattering them like clay pots, as I also have received of my Father;

False idol worship often involved orgies, male and female cult prostitution, and any number of sexual acts of false worship. This church was overlooking the behavior of their members, who were claiming to be part of the church, but then also participating in sexualized acts of worship and idol sacrifices. They perhaps looked at them as fun and/or harmless - they believed in Yahweh, so in their view, it was ok if they also did the fun religious stuff that the majority of their friends and neighbors did. Maybe they just wanted to be tolerant, or did not want to be ostracized, for not joining in, or at least honoring, the other pagan or religious rituals.

We certainly do this now, too afraid to confront other Christians when they commit acts of idolatry, such as consulting psychics, or celebrating holidays devoted to other gods and religions. Some people go to church every week, but also party at the club every weekend, dancing with strangers, because 'Jesus drank wine'. Or maybe it is not even that sinister and obvious. Most of the time, we do not realize when we are being caught in both worlds.

We may be dedicated to church, volunteering, talking about Jesus with others. Then we get invited to a relative's bachelor party, or a co-workers Diwali celebration. We are pressured to go, because we don't want to be rude, or seem like a stick in the mud. Or, we gluttonously over-indulge at the buffet, while people are dying of malnutrition, yet claim to live like Jesus. We have to learn to behave in a way that shows our dedication to following Christ, and is obedient to our Father. We cannot serve two masters. We cannot go to services for other religions, dabble in fortune telling, or celebrate sexual (or any other) immorality. The more freedom you allow the Holy Spirit to grow within you and change your heart, the more uncomfortable you will feel in those situations. You cannot claim to be the church, and then participate in, and celebrate, idolatry and sin. We have to pray and ask for His help to overcome these societal temptations.

In Revelation 3:1-5, He tells the church at Sardis:

> I know your works, that you have a reputation of being alive, but you are dead. Wake up and strengthen the things that remain, which you were about to throw away, for I have found no works of yours perfected before my God. Remember therefore how you have received and heard. Keep it and repent. If therefore you won't watch, I will come as a thief, and you won't know what hour I will come upon you. Nevertheless you have a few names in Sardis that didn't defile their garments. They will walk with me in white, for they are worthy. He who overcomes will be arrayed in white garments, and I will in no way blot his name out of the book of life, and I will confess his name before my Father, and before his angels.

This one probably most easily applies to many of us. We claim to be followers of Christ. We go to church regularly, and help out at the food bank, so we seem to be 'alive' in Christ. However, when God examines our hearts, He may find that many of them are dead. This church, like many of us now, are going through the motions, but not winning souls for Yahweh. These are what some might call 'Christians in name only'. They proclaim their belief loudly, but then do nothing God asks His children to do. They still live the same lifestyle as before they met Christ, with no evidence of being transformed by the Holy Spirit. Are the fruits of the Spirit evident in your life? Are you alive in Christ, or dead in the world? If you didn't tell them, would anyone know you are a Christian, just by observing how you behave?

> To Philadelphia, He says:
>
> I know your works (behold, I have set before you an open door, which no one can shut), that you have a little power, and kept my word, and didn't deny my name. Behold, I make some of the synagogue of Satan, of those who say they are Jews, and they are not, but lie—behold, I will make them to come and worship before your feet, and to know that I have loved you. Because you kept my command to endure, I also will keep you from the hour of testing which is to come on the whole world, to test those who dwell on the earth. I am coming quickly! Hold firmly that which you have, so that no one takes your crown. He who overcomes, I will make him a pillar in the temple of my God, and he will go out from there no more. I will write on him the name of my God and the name of the city of my God, the new Jerusalem, which comes down out of heaven from my God, and my own new name. He who has an ear, let him hear what the Spirit says to the assemblies. (Revelation 3:8-13)

These people have endured and been faithful. He encourages them to continue to endure, and to hold onto their faith. He lets them know that if they cling tightly to every word of God, and stay focused on their mission, they will be rewarded in eternity. This is a lesson to us to always be conscious that we are children of the King, and we must not let anyone take our crown from us. Remember who your Father is, and let His strength fill you, so you can endure anything that is thrown at you.

Lastly, the church at Laodicea is told:

> I know your works, that you are neither cold nor hot. I wish you were cold or hot. So, because you are lukewarm, and neither hot nor cold, I will vomit you out of my mouth. Because you say, 'I am rich, and have gotten riches, and have need of nothing,' and don't know that you are the wretched one, miserable, poor, blind, and naked; I counsel you to buy from me gold refined by fire, that you may become rich; and white garments, that you may clothe yourself, and that the shame of your nakedness may not be revealed; and eye salve to anoint your eyes, that you may see. As many as I love, I reprove and chasten. Be zealous therefore, and repent. Behold, I stand at the door and knock. If anyone hears my voice and opens the door, then I will come in to him and will dine with him, and he with me. He who overcomes, I will give to him to sit down with me on my throne, as I also overcame and sat down with my Father on his throne. He who has an ear, let him hear what the Spirit says to the assemblies." (Revelation 3:15-22)

Once again, this sounds like a familiar plight of many modern-day churches. They focus more on obtaining the wealth of this world, than on bringing brothers and sisters into a right relationship with the Lord. People sit in church every Sunday, hearing the same stories and truths repeated over and over again, and then they go home, turn on the football game, or head to the shops, and life goes right back to normal. If nothing changes in your life, if you become a complacent church that is half in and half out, you are not serving God. He wants us all in, fully dedicated, with evidence of that dedication clear to everyone who comes in contact with us. We need to be on fire for God, not lukewarm. We must pray for His help to increase the fruits of the Spirit in our lives. We must hunger for more of Him, more peace, more love, more joy, more faith. We must consume the Bread of Life, rather than consuming the things of this world.

The church exists because of people. If churches as an entity, and the beliefs they espouse, change based on the people in charge, that is a big red flag. No human should be making up new spiritual or religious rules for people to follow. All teachings, and all authority for those teachings, should come from only one place. God. God Himself left us His words in the Bible as our guide. When we invite the Holy Spirit to live within us, He writes His laws onto our hearts and helps us learn how to obey them. Each denomination, and each individual church, is only as strong as the faith of the people who make it up.

As I have pointed out, this is why it is important to know God's Word and to feel comfortable questioning any religious leader about their basis for something that seems to conflict with the Bible. If they do not have or know the answer, they should pray about your question, then search for the answer in the Bible, ideally together with you. Any religious leader who dismisses or discourages your sincere questions, should be viewed with suspicion. We should all freely ask, until we understand the answers, so that we are ready with the answers when people question us about our faith. Nothing has the potential to cause more damage than a Christian who has no firm root in what the Scriptures say. The elders of the church should be serving everyone else. They should be focused on teaching, answering the earnest questions of newer people, and ensuring the flock they shepherd have a firm understanding of their faith. Their job should not be about making rules, or gaining prestige.

The hierarchies of many church denominations, and the politics involved, are unreal. The enemy planted this idea that laymen cannot teach other laymen. We are all called upon to share our faith. University degrees, certificates, and titles were invented by humans as a means of gate-keeping, and creating artificial barriers to discipleship. Anyone can share the News with anyone. You do not need a long list of credentials, or important-sounding letters after your name, so long as you know and study the Bible, and have a relationship with the Lord. It is crucial to ensure that you are not teaching false doctrine. We see that many of the original disciples were not educated either, "Now when they saw the boldness of Peter and John, and had perceived that they were unlearned and ignorant men, they marveled. They recognized that they had been with Jesus." (Acts 4:13) Through the Holy Spirit, and our relationship with the Lord, we can gain the wisdom to speak well beyond our earthly station.

If you desire to move beyond one on one discipleship, to be a pastor or group leader, check your heart to make sure your motives are pure. Are you filled with a desire to be a servant, and help others find Christ, or are you looking to seem important and well-liked? It is written, "Let not many of you be teachers, my brothers, knowing that we will receive heavier judgment. For we all stumble in many things. Anyone who doesn't stumble in word is a perfect person, able to bridle the whole body also." (James 3:1-2)

This is one of the reasons I find writing these books or going on the radio so intense. I want to make sure I am consulting with the Holy Spirit, and connected to God, so that I do not misrepresent His truth. Thus, I try, and we all must do our best, to ensure we are not attempting to change what God has told us, so that it fits our own ideas about how life should work. Simply stick to His Word. If you do not understand something, ask! Pray about it, and seek His wisdom until you find the answer. I know I will make mistakes, but I do not want to speak or write something that is not true, and mislead potentially thousands of people to their ruin.

There is nothing wrong with studying theology, or earning degrees in Biblical studies, but it is not required in order to be able to share the Good News with others. Many people need that structure and support to help them learn and understand the Bible, and most programs also study the historical and cultural context underlying the events. Thus, earning these credentials can dramatically strengthen the foundation of a believer, and help you learn how to shepherd other believers.

However, plenty of people have a strong academic knowledge of the Bible, and have learned how to give a rousing sermon, but they themselves have not believed its truth in their hearts, or allowed it to change them. No credentials can make up for the power of the Holy Spirit. When we focus too much on human-created degrees, we can end up with people who preach to others, but then commit the darkest of sins in secret. If you are called by God to pastor a church or lead a group, you must obey Him, and not cater to the whims of other humans. Your teaching should be born naturally out of a desire to love God, and love people.

The church is made up of all the people. It is more than one man, or one board of elders. Keep in mind those at the 'top' must be the lowest, most humble of servants. The problem with many churches is that they seem to place substantial reliance on the humans in charge, elevating their leaders to almost deity-like levels. Elders must be knowledgeable and experienced in the faith, and adhere to God's Word. They should not invent new rules and rituals, judge and oppress other members, or seek their own glory and admiration.

Each believer within the church has a duty to serve God, and to help support the purposes of the church. No one person can be a church, no matter how many hours they devote. It takes a group, all working together, with the sole and explicit purpose of obeying, serving, and worshiping Yahweh. Each member should be there to grow spiritually closer to God, and to help others do the same, not to stress about what to wear, how much our neighbor puts into the collection, who is singing that day, or how long the service will be. We should be learning together about the Bible, the evidence that has been discovered of its truth, and methods of discipleship, so we can go out confidently, and share the joy we have found with others. Jesus taught people carefully, and then He taught them how to share what they learned with other people. This is what we are also called to do: learn, and share.

A church building is not required for worshiping God, nor is it required for being saved, or for learning His Word. In fact there is no religious ritual required to be saved other than this: Believe in Yahweh, the God of Abraham. Admit that you have sinned and need help. Repent. Ask for forgiveness, and thank Christ who died to save you. Seek and invite the Holy Spirit to dwell within you. Surrender and let Him cleanse you. Believe. Admit. Repent. Ask. Thank. Seek. Surrender. If you think a specific church membership, or a bunch of hoopla is required, I refer you to the other man being crucified next to Jesus. He went from being a dying criminal and unbeliever, mocking Jesus, to believing, repenting, and asking forgiveness to be with Jesus, all in one day. He was unable to move or perform any rituals. He simply had a complete change of heart, and gave his soul to the Father.

If that is the case, should we still have church buildings? I believe we should, if possible, because they can serve as a place to bring curious friends, and to grow the faithful. Most people are reluctant, or even afraid, to read the Bible, feeling that it will be too challenging to understand, or that they will discover that their situation is hopeless. This is why churches spend a lot of time teaching the lessons contained within the pages of the Bible. Helping people understand what they read can help them see the light, as we see in the example in Acts 8:30-36, of an important Ethiopian eunuch from the court of Queen Candace:

> Philip ran to him, and heard him reading Isaiah the prophet, and said, "Do you understand what you are reading?" He said, "How can I, unless someone explains it to me?" He begged Philip to come up and sit with him. Now the passage of the Scripture which he was reading was this, "He was led as a sheep to the slaughter. As a lamb before his shearer is silent, so he doesn't open his mouth. In his humiliation, his judgment was taken away. Who will declare His generation? For his life is taken from the earth." The eunuch answered Philip, "Who is the prophet talking about? About himself, or about someone else?" Philip opened his mouth, and beginning from this Scripture, preached to him about Jesus. As they went on the way, they came to some water; and the eunuch said, "Behold, here is water. What is keeping me from being baptized?"

In addition to teaching the Bible, I assert the role of every church should be: to encourage everyone to accept Christ's salvation; to support and shepherd the faithful on this journey of life; to go out into the community and serve as Jesus did, spreading the light of God throughout the world; and to come together often to celebrate in thanksgiving, praise, and worship of the magnificence of our Almighty Father. The underlying goal, as individuals, and as the church, should be to love God with our whole being, and to love people, by sharing the news of their salvation. Every other single act of commitment and obedience God asks us to do, is designed to further that goal.

Step one is to teach people about their salvation and the Word of God. People need help understanding the old-fashioned wording, and the historical background underlying the events. In order for us as the church to help people who are new to the faith, and who do not know God's Word, such people have to be welcome to come in and hear the message. They also need to know that the people in the church were sinners too. If the church does not welcome everyone in to learn about God's Word, and if people cannot be open and honest about their own journey with the Lord, then it risks being merely a social club. Newcomers need to feel comfortable that the other humans in the church are not going to judge them for their sins, because they were also once sinners. To that end, we should all be open about sharing our personal journeys with one another.

We must be cautious not to make newcomers feel unwelcome or looked down upon, even if they are doing things we would not consider appropriate. Those who are believers and leaders already within the church are held to a different standard. They should know God's word well enough to help shepherd new people who wander in, looking for hope, not be apprehensive about newcomers. Rather than fear new visitors to our churches, we must teach them how to seek God for themselves, and call them to do so.

We handle the unbeliever and believer differently because of the state they are in. For example, if you see someone drowning in the middle of the lake, that is not the time to give them a swimming lesson. You have to first throw them a life preserver, or some other means of rescue. Unbelievers have to be saved before they can learn how to properly swim and navigate these dangerous waters. The need to find Jesus, and be filled with the Spirit, so they can understand what sin is, and examine their own lives.

We were all sinners before we were saved, and if we are saved, we remember we were once sinners. We still make mistakes, and we have to repent, return to God, and learn from our mistakes. We must pray to Him to help us overcome the temptations that lead us to make these mistakes, so that we stop making them forever. We need His help to resist them, and so do new believers. We did not have to clean ourselves up before we found Christ, and neither do they. As the church, we have to be mindful of where we started, and meet others wherever they currently are on their journey. We have to share the Good News with them, so they can be cleansed, rather than require them to clean up their mess on their own, or condemn them for the dirt they bring with them.

This is slightly different from how we address our own sinfulness, and that of other believers. It is ok to have accidentally ended up in the middle of the lake, drowning, having once been a sinner. It is not ok to intentionally keep diving back in, headfirst, after you have been saved. In other words, you cannot continue to intentionally be a sinner after you accept Jesus. As John the Baptist said, we must "produce fruit worthy of repentance". Once we have accepted Christ's salvation, this means we have agreed with Him that our sins are wrong, and that we understand they keep us separated from God. Thus, we agree to submit to sanctification, learning how to let go of our sinful desires and ways.

Once someone has become a believer, the church's next role is to guide and shepherd the Lord's faithful sheep. We must offer support and admonishment to other believers, our brothers and sisters, as they struggle with their own temptations, just as we need them to do for us. We can pray together, asking God to pull out the roots of all of the anger, lust, greed, pride, and other evil that is clogging up our hearts. Our desire to sin, and to seek the things of this world, should leave us, as we grow closer to God. We should see and feel a difference when we have accepted Christ, and are filled with the Holy Spirit. It should change us from the inside, and manifest on the outside. We should have the fruits of the Spirit, and they should be evident in our daily lives.

In 2 Chronicles 33:3-6, we read a summary of the various things Judah's King Manasseh did during his reign that were "evil in the Lord's sight":

> For he built again the high places which Hezekiah his father had broken down; and he raised up altars for the Baals, made Asheroth, and worshiped all the army of the sky, and served them. He built altars in Yahweh's house, of which Yahweh said, "My name shall be in Jerusalem forever." He built altars for all the army of the sky in the two courts of Yahweh's house. He also made his children to pass through the fire in the valley of the son of Hinnom. He practiced sorcery, divination, and witchcraft, and dealt with those who had familiar spirits

and with wizards. He did much evil in Yahweh's sight, to provoke him to anger.

As 'the church' we must be working to set the example of Christ. We cannot deliberately go out and do those things God calls evil. Once we have declared ourselves to be followers of Christ, then we become representatives of the company, so to speak. Many companies have policies that prohibit what you can do or say while you are on the clock, and/or wearing their uniform. Once we accept the salvation of Christ and turn ourselves over to the Father, we are always on the clock, and in uniform. People will judge us, and look to us as examples of Christianity, so our behavior can influence their opinion of who God is. You also appear to be condoning and supporting these activities and places. The Lord will judge us to see if we have truly renounced all other gods and sources of help, to follow Him alone. This is by no means simple or easy.

You are going to have to do things like turn down invitations to psychics, or your neighbor's Eid celebration, and other things that will lead you to trouble. Those things might seem like harmless fun to many, but they are dangerous, and God considers them wicked. Some things are outright idol worship, while others can be a slippery slope to sinful behavior. Psychics and other forms of divination all risk opening the door to evil spirits. God is reached through prayer, and the spiritual disciplines, not through tarot cards or crystal balls. You have no idea what people are conjuring up during those types of activities. While you may feel like you can control yourself, because you do not think they are real, you could be putting yourself in danger simply by being there. Celebrating pagan and other holidays dishonors Yahweh, and glorifies false gods.

Our flesh is weaker than we think, and we can be affected more deeply than we realize, when we spend time around sin and idolatry. Jesus dined with the outcasts and sinners, but He did not partake of, or encourage their wicked behavior. He did not patronize the brothels or the bars, but He would bring people out of them. When rescuing a stray sheep, you run back with it to safety, you do not sit down and hang out with it next to the wolves' den. Rescuing sinners does not require you to join in their sin yourself, it requires you to grab their hand, and run with them back to the safety of the Shepherd. You might have to deal with being called a fuddy-duddy, boring, or worse, in order to remain faithful to God. You have to decide whether you care more about the judgment of other people, or the judgment of God.

Coupled with this point, if someone who claims to be a follower of Christ is showing evidence of intentional sin, or you know of sins that another believer is not aware of, it is your job as their brother or sister to help them before they fall off. When our brothers and sisters are struggling, it is our job, as part of the church, to help one another, and support each other in our faith. When things seem overwhelming, we should have brothers and sisters in Christ who can remind us of His power, and help us to find strength in our faith. If we want someone to come after us when we wander off the path, we have to be there for our neighbors when they start heading in the wrong direction.

Take some time to explore the following questions as a mental check to see where you stand in your relationship with the Lord. What motivates you? What do you hope in? What is your system of truth? What reward are you hoping for? Are you praying for an abundance of the things of this world, or are you praying for eternal life with God? Do you just sit and listen to a sermon every week, or are you fully immersed in, and obedient to, His Word? We must seek His help to "be doers", actively living out the instructions contained in God's Word:

> So, then, my beloved brothers, let every man be swift to hear, slow to speak, and slow to anger; for the anger of man doesn't produce the righteousness of God. Therefore, putting away all filthiness and overflowing of wickedness, receive with humility the implanted word, which is able to save your souls. But be doers of the word, and not only hearers, deluding your own selves. For if anyone is a hearer of the word and not a doer, he is like a man looking at his natural face in a mirror; for he sees himself, and goes away, and immediately forgets what kind of man he was. But he who looks into the perfect law of freedom and continues, not being a hearer who forgets but a doer of the work, this man will be blessed in what he does. (James 1:19-25)

Pray that He will help you to break free from the lure of this world and its concerns, so that you can know and understand God's will, and obey Him in your everyday practice.

We must be able to gently correct and admonish our fellow believers, and in turn receive correction and admonishment ourselves, if they or we are making mistakes, either about God's Word, or in our personal lives. If our souls are at risk, we should consider it vital to help one another stay on the narrow path, and hold onto one another when we begin to stray. Many times in scripture, a prophet or a friend will correct someone who has done wrong. For example, when King David committed evil, the prophet Nathan bravely confronted and admonished him. That led to repentance by David, thus saving his soul from dying in his wickedness. God tells us we must love everyone, and if we love someone, we should want to help them recognize their sinfulness, so they can repent and return to Yahweh.

Jesus gives us a procedure for handling the sins of other believers:

> If your brother sins against you, go, show him his fault between you and him alone. If he listens to you, you have gained back your brother. But if he doesn't listen, take one or two more with you, that at the mouth of two or three witnesses every word may be established. If he refuses to listen to them, tell it to the assembly. If he refuses to hear the assembly also, let him be to you as a Gentile or a tax collector. (Matthew 18:15-17)

We do not need to put someone 'on blast' or exclude them. Our goal is not to expose other people's sin to the world. Our goal is to help our brother or sister remember Yahweh's instruction, and stay faithful to the Lord. If someone has hurt you, or you know that the pastor, drummer on the worship team, or any fellow member of your church, is harboring some secret sin that they are not addressing, you have an obligation to speak up.

Start by reaching out to them alone, and kindly talking to them about the danger they are putting their soul in. Ask them if they are facing any struggles or stresses in their life, and give them a chance to open up to you. This is not meant to be a hostile confrontation, or a demand for an apology. Even though you may be the person they have hurt, you are not there to seek vengeance, or make them grovel. You are simply trying to help them recognize their behavior, so they can turn to God for help fighting it. If they realize what they have done and repent, you have fulfilled your duty to your brother or sister. You can offer to be a support for them, someone they can call when they are in need, someone to pray with, and someone who will pray for them.

If, however, they deny their sin, or refuse to listen, you can then bring in other friends to help them see the light. If that does not work, you have one more chance to help them, by bringing them before the church. Notice this is not an inquisition, it is meant to be a corrective help, and we should treat them the same way we would want our friends to treat us if we fall short. Think supportive, corrective, and restorative, not accusatory and condemning. God wants to restore our souls, through the sacrifice of Christ, and the work of the Holy Spirit within us. It is our job to remind our fellow believers of this restoration process, and help them get back on track, not to beat them down. The enemy is already doing their worst to attack our brothers and sisters, and keep them down. They do not need our help. They were our former slave masters, and we used to do their bidding, until Jesus set us free. We cannot go back to working for their side.

We should support one another as we earnestly struggle in our flesh, and help each other remain submitted to the Holy Spirit. However, if someone outright refuses to repent, or to stop deliberately committing transgressions, then He says they should no longer be considered a believer, they are just like a tax collector or gentile (anyone not Jewish). They can no longer hold a position of apparent authority within the church, and should not be considered among the members. You cannot allow the rot of hypocrites to spread, and infect everyone else in the congregation.

Another thing to keep in mind, is that all of this must be done in accordance with God's Word. Jesus told us we must learn to turn the other cheek when someone wrongs us. If you are upset over something that was just a misunderstanding or mistake, consider praying and asking God if it is worth pursuing the matter to this extent. Do I really need to get this worked up over a small mistake? This process was designed for restoration, not petty revenge. You are only to bring up occasions where your brother has sinned against you, not every single random dispute. Check your motives. Are you worried about their soul, or your own pride and concerns?

We must not forget that before we can do any of this, we have to start with ourselves, and our own sins, first. We have talked at length in the previous books about not judging others. We recall that in Matthew 7:5 Jesus told us:

> Why do you see the speck that is in your brother's eye, but don't consider the beam that is in your own eye? Or how will you tell your brother, 'Let me remove the speck from your eye,' and behold, the beam is in your own eye? You hypocrite! First remove the beam out of your own eye, and then you can see clearly to remove the speck out of your brother's eye.

We need to spend time with the Holy Spirit going through sanctification, before we can even begin to start worrying about the flaws in others. Jesus makes it clear that if we do see a flaw in someone, it does not make us any better than them, because we likely have a much bigger, more obvious flaw.

We grow so used to our own bad behavior, we don't even notice it anymore. We have to ask for help to make us aware of, and remove, our own 'beams' that are impairing our ability to see clearly. If we have not yet fully surrendered to Christ, and experienced the peace and joy that come with salvation, how could we share it with others? We need our own story of transformation to share when we tell people how good the Lord is. There must be evidence when we claim He has changed us. We have to pray for every root of bitterness and sin to be pulled from our hearts, no matter what that takes, or how painful it is to give up.

A third purpose of the church is service. Church members should be a light in the communities they are in, sharing God's love with the world through their outreach. We are directed to take care of, and provide help to those in need, as in the example Jesus gave in Luke 10:25-37:

> Behold, a certain lawyer stood up and tested him, saying, "Teacher, what shall I do to inherit eternal life?" He said to him, "What is written in the law? How do you read it?" He answered, "You shall love the Lord your God with all your heart, with all your soul, with all your strength, and with all your mind; and your neighbor as yourself." He said to him, "You have answered correctly. Do this, and you will live." But he, desiring to justify himself, asked Jesus, "Who is my neighbor?" Jesus answered, "A certain man was going down from Jerusalem to Jericho, and he fell among robbers, who both stripped him and beat him, and departed, leaving him half dead. By chance a certain priest was going down that way. When he saw him, he passed by on the other side. In the same way a Levite also, when he came to the place and saw him, passed by on the other side. But a certain Samaritan, as he traveled, came where he was. When he saw him, he was moved with compassion, came to him, and bound up his wounds, pouring on oil and wine. He set him on his own animal, brought him to an inn, and took care of him. On the next day, when he departed, he took out two denarii, gave them to the host, and said to him, 'Take care of him. Whatever you spend beyond that, I will repay you when I return.' Now which of these three do you think seemed to be a neighbor to him who fell among the robbers?" He said, "He who showed mercy on him." Then Jesus said to him, "Go and do likewise."

Priests and Levites were supposed to be the ones who set the perfect example of righteousness. Samaritans were looked down upon. Jesus shows us, yet again, that looking perfect and righteous in public does not matter, if we ignore our neighbor in need when we think no one is watching. If we truly believe in

God, we know He is always watching. We know what He wants us to do when we see someone in need. We cannot claim to be obedient to God if we allow others to suffer, and do nothing meaningful to help.

Helping those in need is not just about handing out money, or donations of food and supplies, although that can be beneficial. We know that if a person's basic needs are not met, their focus will be on that, and they will struggle to pay attention to anything else. Jesus fed and healed people when He shared the Word with them. Sometimes we have to help our neighbors free up space in their minds from worry over their survival, in order for them to be able to listen and be attentive to God's voice calling them.

This is why most church outreach includes the meeting of basic needs, such as food and clothing pantries, delivering meals, providing bus passes and shelter, etc. However, the meeting of physical needs, while helpful, is not as valuable as meeting spiritual needs. We want to make sure we are not just enabling people to continue to wallow in misery and sin, but that our help is coupled with sharing God's love with them. Along with the meal or supplies, we must provide information about how they can be saved and healed too.

We need to make sure when we hand out meals to people, that we also talk to them and let them know that they are children of the Father, and He wants better for them. We let them know how they can find the Bread of Life and Living Water, so they will never be hungry or thirsty again. We let people know where their help is coming from. We make it clear that the assistance we give is not from us, but from their Father in Heaven who loves them. Helping others is not something we do to glorify ourselves, but to glorify God.

When time spent volunteering overtakes time with the Lord, you might have to take a step back and examine your motives. Being on the cleaning committee, the worship team, and coordinating every holiday potluck are all great things to do, but the outcome of our efforts should lead to saving souls, not just making friends. We do not want to volunteer solely for the sake of keeping busy, winning admiration, or appearing to be martyrs of our time. Our job is to spread the news, not plan the perfect church picnic. When we lose focus on the Lord, our business in these good works can become a way to escape, or hide ourselves from truly opening up to the Holy Spirit.

Finally, the church is a place where believers can gather together to celebrate and give thanks! We have so much to be thankful for: God's love for us, Christ's sacrifice to save us, the miraculous healing we have received through the Holy Spirit, and the millions of other miracles experienced by believers each day, not to mention eternal life!! We can rejoice and be glad in the Lord, singing praises to the Father, worshiping together. We can deepen our relationship with Him, and feel His presence, when we worship with others, as Jesus said in Matthew 18:20, "For where two or three are gathered together in my name, there I am in the middle of them." Times spent like this renew our spirits in gladness, and fortify us to go out into the world to share that jubilation with others.

We are sent out to the wolves. Much of this world rejects God, and fights against us. We will stand a better chance of resisting the enemy, and obeying God's commands, when we know there are others supporting us, and believing with us. It is comforting to know that there are other humans who will stand with us. Our heartfelt worship and fellowship with other believers fills us with God's strength. More importantly, as we grow closer to Christ through our communion and worship, we find the true power is knowing that even if one day there are no other believers with us, we can be assured that God, and the full army of Heaven, are always standing nearby.

Being the church requires positive, deliberate action on our part. We should remember we cannot become standoffish, closed away secretly in our church buildings. We cannot become exclusionary, keeping God's promises, and the news of salvation, to ourselves. We must be the salt of the earth and a beacon to those in need, sharing God's light and love with the entire world. We must remember our love of Jesus Christ, and remove all false idols from our midst. We must bolster one another's faith, and support each other when we are in need. We must act as God's hands and feet here on Earth. When we pray that His will be done, we are basically asking Him to guide us, to do whatever it is His will for us to do. We are essentially praying that we will be made capable of doing His will. We can no longer be pew-sitters, we have to be go-getters!

NOTES

4

The Great Commission

"Therefore don't be afraid of them, for there is nothing covered that will not be revealed, or hidden that will not be known. What I tell you in the darkness, speak in the light; and what you hear whispered in the ear, proclaim on the housetops."

- Matthew 10:26-27

"Declare his glory among the nations, his marvelous works among all the peoples."

- Psalm 96:3

Imagine you were recently visited by an attorney, who had some exciting, but very urgent news. Like a storyline out of a movie, a distant family member, whom you didn't know existed, passed away, leaving a huge fortune. The attorney for the departed was searching records, and tracked you and your siblings down as the sole surviving heirs to the estate, but there is one problem. The inheritance will be released to the state if the heirs do not come forward by midnight. They are going to take everyone via helicopter to the courthouse, because they are required to appear in person to claim it. Everyone has been rounded up, except the attorney cannot seem to get in contact with one of your brothers. He is not answering his phone, door, email, or messages.

It's getting down to the wire for him to have enough time to join you on the flight, and claim his share of the estate. You suddenly realize what is going on. There is a virtual reality game you both used to play. You stopped playing after a while, because it was starting to become too time-consuming, but you know he still plays. He must be down in his basement, with his headset on, immersed in the action. You know he can't hear anything outside of the game. You always warned him the house would burn down without him noticing.

You know that you are the only person with the knowledge and ability to reach him. You are the only one who stands a chance at connecting with him through the game, to tell him the news. You remember his username, and you quickly hop on, jump into the in-game chat, and tell him he has to hurry up, run upstairs and go see this attorney who is at the door. He is angry with you for interrupting him right in the middle of a crucial part of his game. He is about to accomplish a major victory, so he tells you to be quiet and hold on. You ignore him, and tell him what is going on, but he is screaming over you, or barely listening, so focused on the game. He might even mute you. Or if he does listen, he thinks you are pranking him.

You start telling him it's an emergency, because you know that whatever fun he thinks he is having in the game, is nothing compared to how excited he is going to be when he hears the news. You ask him if he has read his messages, and he says he hasn't had time to check them. His team has been running dungeon raids all day long, seeking the ultimate rare drop of in-game treasure. They are counting on him, and they're so close. He can't quit now. If they pull this off, they will have more in-game gold than they know what to do with.

You say everything you can to convince him you are telling the truth. The choice is up to him. Will he quit the game at this crucial point, take off the headset, and join in the real-life inheritance, or will he miss his chance chasing virtual wealth? No one can make him do anything. Just as no one can force anyone else to listen to the Gospel, or welcome the Holy Spirit. No one can force anyone else to give up chasing the imaginary, temporary wealth of this world, in order to receive their eternal inheritance.

The brother might decide that giving up the game to take a risk, and answer the door, is too much to ask right now. He is caught up in fighting an imaginary battle, and he is in deep. His online friends are counting on him, and they have been there for him when he was feeling low. When his family was annoyed with him, and wouldn't pick up the phone, these online friends were there for him. When he was stressed out or upset, he could log into the game and be greeted warmly by them. He could forget his problems, and be distracted by the imaginary world of his game. In that world, he was important, a leader, powerful, well-respected, and liked.

No one in his family understands how important the game, and these people, are to him. They have shared important moments in each other's lives, and gotten to know one another, over years of playing together. Their guild is at the top of the charts right now, and they run like a well-oiled machine. Most of the time, the game, and these people, feel more loving than his own family, and more real and normal than this world.

As we have discussed in *Pursuit to Commitment*, giving up the very real, very comfortable pleasures of this world is extremely difficult. Humans in general hate change. We tend to gravitate toward things that are familiar and easy. There is nothing better than coming home after a rough day, and indulging in our favorite relaxation activity. For some, it is gaming. For others it might be things like food, scrolling social media, tv shows, sex, or alcohol. The thought of switching up even something minor in our daily routine, or giving up our comforts, can make us anxious and uneasy. Convincing someone to switch up their entire spiritual belief paradigm can seem nearly impossible. No matter how open-minded we claim to be, we are generally unwilling to consider different or opposing ideas. We tend to plug our ears, and close our eyes to anything that contradicts what we think we know.

To anyone who is still sitting in their basement with their headphones on, anyone who cannot hear Jesus knocking at the door, our job as their brother or sister is to jump into the chat to make contact with them. God can use our unique relationships, or talents, to reach particular people, and establish open communication. We can let them know Someone important is at the door, and they need to go answer it. If we let Him in when He knocks on the door of our heart, and we listen to His good news, we will get to share in His fortune. You don't have to clean up the house first, or even pack your bags. Simply invite Him in, and He will help you.

I, and all believers, should be out every day sharing the news of God, and the sacrifice of Jesus Christ. We should be telling everyone we meet about the Holy Spirit so that they can be saved too. What is stopping us? For me, it was fear. I was so terrified of how people would judge me for my faith, that at first, I was afraid to even tell anyone. Even after completing the first book, I was nervous and awkward about sharing it with others. I prayed every day for help overcoming that fear of judgment and rejection. One thing that helped, was remembering that the message is not about me, it is about God.

As the saying goes, "I am just one beggar, trying to tell another beggar where to find food." One of our most important roles is to share the Gospel with others. In fact it is what we are meant to devote ourselves to, and give our lives for. The objective of disciples is to fulfill the Great Commission Jesus gave when He left. We are to give our lives in exchange for other people, just as Christ did. While of course we cannot save their souls the way Christ did, it is our job to tell them about Him, and to try to help them understand His message.

It was difficult at first for me to understand why we need to give our lives for people. Until I more deeply realized this truth: everything else in this world that we currently live for, will be gone one day. This includes your money, car, house, schooling, job, clothes, jewelry, all of your possessions. When we are laid to rest, someone else takes it all. Furthermore, in the end, everything on Earth will be burned. Nothing we purchase, or spend our lives worrying about, lasts forever. The only earthly things that last are people. God's Word, and our souls, are eternal, which is why those are the things we should devote our lives to.

Once you are devoted to God, and to sharing the News, you notice how silly it is to be consumed with material things. None of it lasts. None of it brings meaning or purpose to our lives. People throughout time, and even now, all over the world, live without many of the things we cling to, and still live perfectly well. The person living in the small run-down shack is just as likely to be living a happy, fulfilled, life as the person living in the mansion. In fact, they could even be more likely to find peace and joy, if their humble lifestyle means they do not have the stress of having to work long hours, or be away from their families, just to afford the mansion. I feel so much less pressure since the Holy Spirit has helped me to stop worrying about buying things, and impressing others. Money does not matter; we do not need it to exist. If we instead focus on helping people find the Lord, we learn how much more fulfilling that purpose is.

Later in this book, we will look at the role overwhelming compulsions play as a form of obedience, but I wanted to share one quick example here. It was a time when the Holy Spirit gave me insight to our role in the Great Commission, in the form of a sudden compulsion. I was washing dishes one day, and God made me stop, take off my gloves, and write these sentences down: This book, and all other books about God, are not designed to force you to commit to God. No one can make anyone else believe or do anything. Even with a gun to your head, the choice is always yours. Only you can make the decision to follow God.

Every pastor, author, songwriter, messenger, or friend can only tell you what we know, and have experienced with God, in the hopes it will get you curious. Maybe you will want to see if you can find what we have - the peace that comes from knowing God. In Revelation 3:20, Jesus says, "Behold, I stand at the door and knock. If anyone hears my voice and opens the door, then I will come in to him and will dine with him, and he with me." We cannot force anyone to open the door to Jesus, but we must do whatever we can to help them hear His knock, encourage them to answer the door, and invite Him in. We cannot sit back and allow our brothers and sisters to miss out on their inheritance, without at least trying to get through to them.

If you discovered the cure for a disease, or found some method that actually worked to relieve back pain, you would probably share that information with everyone you knew who suffered from that affliction. So, since we have found the cure for sin, the Way that actually leads to healing and salvation, why aren't we sharing that news with everyone? More than just a temporary disease or pain, their souls are in danger of eternal damnation in the pit of fire. It is urgent that we each share the Good News that we have been saved, and help others learn about their salvation, before it is too late. When we are filled with the Holy Spirit, we feel the pull to share the faith with others. If we do not share, we are not obeying God.

Who should we share our faith with? As Jesus told the disciples in Matthew 28:19-20, :

> Go and make disciples of all nations, baptizing them in the name of the Father and of the Son and of the Holy Spirit, teaching them to observe all things that I commanded you. Behold, I am with you always, even to the end of the age." Amen.

Everyone is welcome to hear the Good News. Jesus says that ALL nations should be taught the truth, so that disciples could be made from every country. The Lord will save everyone who believes in Him, and calls upon Him with their whole heart. However, if no one ever shares the information with them, how will they learn about it? Thus, many disciples were commissioned by Jesus to share it with everyone, no matter what their background was. Throughout the entire Bible, we see the Lord calling His people to tell unbelievers about Him. The prophets in the Old Testament had to warn the people to repent and return to Yahweh. The reigns of each king of Israel and Judah were judged, based on whether they directed their subjects to follow the Lord, or to worship false idols. Now it is our turn to continue their work.

God is not at war with human beings. He is at war with evil, and He is saving humans from living with evil forever. We just happen to be fighting alongside evil every single time we utter a mean word to someone, or hurt another person. He invites us all to be soldiers on His side in this war, instead of working for evil. Once we turn ourselves over to Him, we become one more person who is fighting against evil. We fight evil by reflecting God's light onto it, so people can see who and what they have been fighting for. One of the greatest jobs we have as believers, is to bring along as many people as we can, by infiltrating enemy ranks to recruit our fellow humans to switch sides. We need more people fighting on the side of good, and battling evil with us. The war is happening right now, for real. Jump into the fray and help pull your brothers and sisters out of darkness, and over to the winning side.

In Matthew 9:36-38, we read of how Jesus was concerned for the lack of people working to share the News:

> But when he saw the multitudes, he was moved with compassion for them because they were harassed and scattered, like sheep without a shepherd. Then he said to his disciples, "The harvest indeed is plentiful, but the laborers are few. Pray therefore that the Lord of the harvest will send out laborers into his harvest."

Jesus is going to come one day soon to collect the harvest, the living and the dead who believe in Him. It is our job to work as His laborers in the field, 'harvesting' more of our brothers and sisters. Then we are asked to serve as shepherds, supporting them on their faith walk, helping them learn, until they are also ready for discipleship. He is saying there is a lot of work to do - the harvest is plentiful. There are billions of lost souls who do not understand or know Yahweh. If there are approximately two billion people in the world who claim to follow Christ, and there are approximately eight billion people currently alive on Earth, this would mean that if each of us was able to teach six people about God, and how Jesus died to save us, and they believed, and surrendered themselves to Him, the whole world would be saved! Imagine how the world would be if we were all in absolute peace and agreement that Jesus Christ is our Lord and Savior! Imagine how we would celebrate in great joy together with all the angels! This is the goal of Heaven!

Fantastic, you think, I will go get my six people right now and I'll be all set! You obviously know it is not going to be that simple. First of all, it takes a lot of work to harvest souls. While the Farmer is watering and adding nutrients to the soil, the rodents are underground gnawing at the roots, and the birds, bugs, disease, and weather threaten the harvest daily. In addition, as Jesus warned, the workers are few. When farmers are harvesting crops, they don't generally have a very long time to get them all in, especially if the weather is a factor. Harvest time is a rushed, busy time in most cases. If there is a shortage of workers, the ones who do show up, are going to have to work extra hard to pick up the slack. They will have to keep working until the job is complete, to ensure that none of the harvest is left behind to be wasted and destroyed.

As mentioned, Jesus is returning soon, on a day and time we do not know. Our window of time to harvest is limited. Out of the two billion self-proclaimed Christians, I would guess quite a lot of them are not doing anything to spread the Word. This means that it is up to you and me to make up for their lack of effort. We should be doing everything we can to reach as many people as we can, as quickly as we can. Don't let the enormity of the task get to you though, simply ask God who He wants you to talk to first, and go from there. Like workers harvesting a field, they focus on picking one plant at a time, and then they move quickly to the next one. If they stop working to look around at how much of the field is left to harvest, they could throw their hands up in despair at the work that remained. Don't watch the clock, or worry about how hard everyone else is working, just keep your eyes on your own work. We have to keep harvesting souls until Jesus returns, or we take our last breath in this life.

The trouble is, it can be intimidating to share our faith. When talking to people about God, you may be met with some mix of hostility, suspicion, annoyance, boredom, curiosity, interest, debate, or agreement. In other words, you never know what you're going to get, so you have to be prepared for anything. People, including myself before I was awakened, have been misled and fed lies about who God is, so we have to be prepared. Most of them do not understand the truth because they have never actually read or heard the truth.

This includes many people who say they believe in Jesus. Again, I was one of these people. I would have said I believed, although my conviction was certainly not firm. I had no idea what the Bible said, so I had no idea what my half-hearted belief meant. I thought the Bible said many things that it doesn't. I definitely did not have the Holy Spirit, and had never allowed Him to change my life. Most people are like that. They believe all kinds of things about God that are not true. You have to understand that, so you can be prepared with the information to correct their mistaken beliefs.

Some people are going to think you are crazy. They are going to call you stupid for believing in a 'magical wizard sky-daddy' instead of trusting human scientists. Take heart, before you professed your faith in God, some people likely secretly already thought you were crazy for some other reason! Seriously though, it is far better to be thought crazy for trusting God, than to deny God because you are worried a few people might think you are crazy. We have to remember to see ourselves as God sees us, not through the eyes of other people.

Even back in Old Testament times, people were laughed at for sharing their faith in God. We read in 2 Chronicles 30:10, about how people reacted when King Hezekiah sent word to the people to return to God, and celebrate Passover, "So the couriers passed from city to city through the country of Ephraim and Manasseh, even to Zebulun, but people ridiculed them and mocked them." This was one of the things I was fearful of when I gave myself back to the Lord. We have to know and understand, no matter how sincere we are, and no matter how much it makes sense to us, most people are walking around blind. To them, we do seem crazy, because they believe science has somehow disproved God. We have to remember that without the Holy Spirit, all of this is difficult to understand, so we have to be patient as we explain.

It is not easy to read mocking or angry comments, but it has been getting easier and easier as my faith and trust have been growing, and my fear and insecurity have been shrinking. In fact, recently, I have found myself feeling sort of exhilarated by those comments. It is as if I can see the hurt and desperation within them. They lash out at what they do not yet understand. I stopped taking their attacks personally, and pray for them instead. Instead of feeling bothered by their remarks, I become eager to sympathize with them, and explain the things they are misunderstanding. I have observed that when I respond respectfully, and ask honest questions, people tend to respond back in a generally positive way. When I ignore their personal slights, and focus on the message, the conversation tends to remain civil. If I respond back with anger or rudeness, it only tends to escalate the animosity. At that point, no one is listening to the substance, they are only focused on the drama.

For those who resort to nothing but vulgar insults, we should just pray for them, and move on. We have to recognize the truth that we cannot make the choice for anyone else. No matter how much you try to get your brother to believe you, and leave the game, the choice ultimately resides with him. Our job is simply to get people to realize Jesus is knocking at the door, and to encourage them to let Him in. If they refuse, they aren't rejecting us, they're rejecting His offer of salvation, and sharing in His fortune. They are willing to risk trading eternity in paradise, to go back to living in their worldly problems. The rewards the brother will get in the game pale in comparison to real life. Just as the rewards we get on Earth pale in comparison to God's heavenly rewards. We just have to do our best to convince them to open their eyes and ears, minds and hearts, to understand the truth.

Some people are not downright hostile to the idea of God, but they are worried about changes they will have to make in their lifestyle. I realized a lot of people simply feel judged by the mere mention of Christ. They equate Christianity with the angry elder at church, or the high school bully, who harassed, and hurt them, thus they blame you for even talking about God. They are so afraid they will discover that they are condemned, and have no hope, that they do not even bother to find out the truth.

Others think they know about the Bible and Christianity, but have clearly never read it well enough to understand. They spout off a cobbled-together version of God's plan, parroting a random mix of what others have said the Bible says, and their own opinions about what it should say. Both those who profess to be believers, and those who do not, can be found spouting off inaccurate statements. They clearly show they do not know God, or comprehend the Bible. Still others admit they do not know anything, and have never bothered to give it much thought. We have to remember that we too were once without knowledge, and we could easily still make mistakes ourselves. This allows us to respond to their questions and misunderstandings with patience and kindness.

We can share our story with all kinds of people, no matter where they currently are on the belief spectrum. This is where we want to remember who we were, before we found Christ. The people we engage with will see us as examples of the faith, and will begin to ask us questions to test the waters. Our evangelism, and our personal testimonies, can really come into play here. When someone is curious about topics in the Bible, we need to encourage that. This means we are either ready with an answer to their questions, or we take a moment to look up the answer with them. This is such a lengthy topic that there are entire books, podcasts, courses, etc. dedicated to apologetics, but I will share some of my thoughts and examples in the next chapter.

We all have to discover our own skill set when it comes to participating in the Great Commission. Each of us has different personalities and communication styles. We have varying comfort levels and abilities, and God wants to use each of our unique strengths to reach out to as many people as possible. For example, some people are more outgoing and thrive as one-on-one evangelists, at work, and with random strangers. I, on the other hand, do a lot more written and family evangelism, working on these books and on some apologetics online. I prefer time to compose my answers. I recommend starting with the style of engagement that you are most comfortable with, and that best suits your skill-set. As God builds your confidence in that area, He may begin to open other arenas for you to work in.

If you invite Him to, He will use your creative, intellectual, and social skills to reach specific people. There will be something about the way you explain it, that suddenly hits them differently. You will have an ability to help them make a connection, or understand God's plan in a way they never have before. Maybe you get your big chance, and almost everyone ignores you. Perhaps there is just one person you personally reach when you share the News. But what if that one person ends up bringing hundreds, or even thousands, of people to Christ? What if the only reason they did so was because God set it up, by placing you in their path to share the Gospel with them? Maybe they read an article, or a comment you wrote, heard a song you performed, or simply worked in the cubicle next to you, and observed your behavior. You do not have to worry about practicing every type of evangelism, or speaking to a million people, just focus on what God has called you to do.

One common way we can start is by sharing our personal experience of how we were saved through Christ, and what God has done in our lives. We generally refer to that as our testimony. Contrary to the popular argument that there is no evidence of God, we have ample evidence in the form of the personal testimonies of people like me. We have fully experienced the dramatic transformation that the Holy Spirit works within us. This does not happen by magic, or with a pill.

Similar to a witness in a trial, our testimony is additional evidence of the truth of God's Word. We are witnesses to His power. If millions and millions of people describe how knowing Jesus transformed and uplifted their lives, it helps to encourage others that the same can happen to them. If we hear about someone who has suffered in ways that are similar to, or worse than what we have, it gives us hope that maybe God can help us. For help describing your own testimony, you can listen to examples of testimonies online, talk to other believers, or read books by various authors.

Our testimonies are the story of our own personal salvation and change. You cannot be a witness to something you have not experienced yourself. In order to have a personal testimony, you have to have met Christ, and submitted to Him. You have to have allowed the Holy Spirit to make dramatic changes in your life. You cannot have a testimony without a transformation. I heard a phrase that explains it well, 'you have to go through the test to get the testimony'. As we saw in *Pursuit to Commitment*, when you repent and return to the Lord, fully giving your soul over to Him, you begin to go through the sanctification process. As you do so, you overcome addictions and strongholds, your attitude shifts, and your heart and mind begin to change. You grow stronger and more obedient, conforming to Yahweh's original flawless design. You have firsthand, eyewitness testimony to the power of God in your life. You can share with others about the freedom you have experienced because of the sacrifice of Jesus, and your sacrifice of your own life to Him.

If you haven't yet repented and submitted to the Almighty Father, and accepted Christ, then you may be able to share and explain the Gospel, but you do not necessarily have what is traditionally referred to as a testimony. This is because you have not yet had the first-hand experience of a relationship with Him. I urge you to seek Him and repent right away, and invite the Holy Spirit to fill you completely, if you have not already done so. Then submit to the refinery of sanctification, and begin the process of purging the contamination of wickedness out of you.

When I first began exploring my faith, it seemed to me that the most popular testimonies I would hear were of two types: 1) those whom God saved from extreme abuse, trauma, or illness, or 2) those whom God helped overcome debilitating addictions, criminal pasts, homelessness, etc. These are the people who make great motivational speakers. They are the perfect, interesting stories to put on a video, or in a book if you want to inspire people. After all, if God can turn around the life of a man who stabbed someone, or a woman who was homeless and addicted to heroin, the rest of us should be easy, right? These testimonies can give us great hope if we take the lessons they learned, and apply them to our own lives.

We have to be cautious though, because those extraordinary types of testimonies can also inadvertently create problems. I remember, when I would hear these sensational testimonies, prior to making the leap, I would feel so sorry for them, and the abuse they suffered. Or I would feel so amazed at the willpower it took for them to overcome, and turn their lives around. I did not make any immediate connections to my own life, because I did not relate to their circumstances. I also did not make the right connections to God's involvement, because I saw these as dramatic rescues of people in desperate need, which I did not think applied to my situation. I saw them as something that had never happened to me, and likely never would. I did not see my own desperate need for a savior reflected in their experiences.

In my mind, their stories were more of an entertainment, or wow factor, than an example of how to grow my own faith. Their situations seemed so extreme and far-removed from my so-called 'normal' life, that I did not see the (now obvious) parallels. This meant that the lessons they learned, while extremely valuable to them, were not as straightforwardly applicable to my own situation. We each need to hear from people who come from similar circumstances, or have similar doubts and struggles to our own.

Our testimonies shouldn't be about making people feel sorry for us, or about giving us some kind of clout because they're sensational. We have to resist the urge to fall into that trap. When giving your testimony, keep the focus on what God did in your life, and how He rescued you. This is not about your own actions. Whatever you do, do not make yourself the hero of your testimony. You got yourself into the messes you were in, it was only because of God's grace and mercy that He got you out.

As He grew my knowledge and understanding, I began to embrace the power of testimony, even while my own was being built. I realized that very few people spoke openly of the everyday type of sins they themselves had committed, and how God had forgiven them for those things. Every saint who is in Christ, has a powerful testimony of how He saved them from their sinfulness. Overcoming abuse and disease, or a criminal past, are testimonies that really give us a sense of God's miracle-power to heal us. But it is just as inspiring to hear stories of 'normal', boring people. Stories of people who learned to seek God in line at the grocery store, as well as at the big game, and the changes that He brought, can speak to people in a way that more of us can relate to.

We have to learn that our testimony is valuable because it helps us to teach and reach people in a way they can understand. We have to help them learn about God's word, and show them how it applied to our lives in a practical, immediate way, as well as in a spiritual, eternal way. We are able to speak the same language, we share the same experiences, we know the way to the minds and hearts of the people around us. This means we can talk to them in a way that no one else could.

Someone working on a farm is going to feel more comfortable with someone who shares similar concerns, and can relate to them. They can use their common background to help them understand God's plans, in the same way that the person with the country club membership may learn best from someone who understands their lifestyle. If someone wealthy comes to God and gives up their sinfulness, yet still has access to, and knows the lingo of, other wealthy people, they are a perfect worker in that field. The neurosurgeon is not as likely to take the time to listen to the random street preacher, as she will another surgeon. We all have our specialty and our niche for a reason.

I do enjoy and get emotional hearing powerful testimony, but I am here to strongly advocate for the rest of us to get out there, and share our seemingly normal, boring testimonies with the people around us. If our general experiences really are normal, doesn't that by definition mean that the average person will relate more closely to our experiences, than they will relate to those of a prisoner, or victim of sex trafficking? Our own issues can be the hardest to see. If I have reached a point where I can tell you plainly about my own flaws and struggles, and how God helps me, and if they are similar to the flaws and struggles you have, it might be more useful to you than a story that is more captivating, but that you cannot identify with at all.

Putting too much emphasis on having a dramatic story can also make the rest of us feel like our own testimonies are not worth sharing. Sometimes, I believe focusing on only sensational testimonies can have the unintended consequence of making the rest of us feel like we do not have anything to be saved from, or to work on, because our lives appear neater or easier. People who learned how to admit that many of their everyday habits and vices are actually sins, holding them back from the beauty of God's love, can help to open our eyes to our own sins.

We should really spend more time and focus on the daily temptations and sins the rest of us deal with, and not always just showcase the movie-worthy stories. I believe judgment comes because we think sinners are only those people who are in jail, or who committed the most outrageous acts. We start to think we are not that bad, so we do not feel an urgency to repent and straighten up. We have to share our own testimony of our 'normal' sins, how Jesus forgave them, and how we have overcome them through sanctification. By doing so, we can help others see their own sins, and their own need for His mercy. Socially acceptable sins are still sins.

We need to be somewhat careful in how we approach people, especially those who do not even consider the slightest possibility that there is an afterlife, or a spiritual realm. For example, if you tell these people that lust is a temptation of the devil, they will look at you like you have four heads. Heck, I'm sure many people who believe they are followers of Christ would do the same. If someone is not filled with the Spirit, actively seeking to know God, and submitted to His service, they will have a very difficult time understanding. They may not be aware of the devil, and his influence on the world. We have to keep that in mind, and meet people where they are currently. Ask questions to figure out what is holding them back from belief, and then do your best to clear up their misconceptions.

Our duty to share the Good News with everyone is a very serious obligation. If they do not repent and seek God, they could be in great danger. It is God's desire that no one should be away from Him and perish, but if we are not working to warn others, that is exactly what could happen:

> You, son of man, tell the house of Israel: 'You say this, "Our transgressions and our sins are on us, and we pine away in them. How then can we live?"' Tell them, "'As I live," says the Lord Yahweh, "I have no pleasure in the death of the wicked, but that the wicked turn from his way and live. Turn, turn from your evil ways! For why will you die, house of Israel?"' (Ezekiel 33:10-11)

You must share this information with others, letting them know that God loves them, and that they still have a chance, if they seek God for themselves. If possible, try to encourage them to repent and receive salvation. So long as you do your best to tell them the truth, and warn them of what will happen if they reject Christ, you have done your job. This is why we are told in Ezekiel 33:8-9:

> When I tell the wicked, 'O wicked man, you will surely die,' and you don't speak to warn the wicked from his way, that wicked man will die in his iniquity, but I will require his blood at your hand. Nevertheless, if you warn the wicked of his way to turn from it, and he doesn't turn from his way; he will die in his iniquity, but you have delivered your soul.

Once you have spent some time learning and walking with the Holy Spirit's guidance, you must tell everyone else what you know. Remember though, that we cannot change anyone. We cannot judge anyone. All we can do is tell them about the Gospel, how Jesus saved our lives, and how we were changed. They must make the choice and surrender. Then we must pray, trust, and believe that God will change them too. The time is short, and the message is urgent. We must each pray for help for all of us, as believers, to overcome whatever obstacles are holding us back from getting out, and telling the world about Him.

Notes

5

Have an Answer

"Behold, I send you out as sheep among wolves. Therefore be wise as serpents and harmless as doves. But beware of men, for they will deliver you up to councils, and in their synagogues they will scourge you. Yes, and you will be brought before governors and kings for my sake, for a testimony to them and to the nations. But when they deliver you up, don't be anxious how or what you will say, for it will be given you in that hour what you will say. For it is not you who speak, but the Spirit of your Father who speaks in you."

- Matthew 10:16-20

Now who will harm you if you become imitators of that which is good? But even if you should suffer for righteousness' sake, you are blessed. "Don't fear what they fear, neither be troubled." But sanctify the Lord God in your hearts. Always be ready to give an answer to everyone who asks you a reason concerning the hope that is in you, with humility and fear, having a good conscience. Thus, while you are spoken against as evildoers, they may be disappointed who curse your good way of life in Christ.

- 1 Peter 3:13-16

Science versus God. History versus God. That is how many people try to frame the discussion. They claim that science and history absolutely contradict what the Bible says. They mock the idea of a worldwide flood, and believe that science has proven things like evolution, or the age of fossils. People who have this faith and trust in science, may believe they are superior to you. They may call you ignorant for believing in creation. This is OK. When you begin to share your faith with others, you will be attacked for it. This is guaranteed. It will not happen every time, but it will happen. As soon as people find out you believe, they will start to question or confront you about these issues, heavily at times. This is because some people need a lot of convincing to believe. God has put them in your path to ask these questions for a reason. Knowing this in advance gives you a chance to be prepared.

To start, I believe we need to stop allowing people to frame the argument as 'science versus the Bible'. God made us in His image. We are intelligent creatures. Humans have a very unique intelligence compared to animals. All animals have intelligence, in that they are able to communicate, often with a complex language system. They know how to solve problems, and perform tasks, within their abilities and needs, and some even use tools, but their intelligence has limits. No animal has ever invented complicated technological devices. A dolphin has never invented an iPad. Humans are different. We can somehow conceive of, and create things, that we have never seen before. We can combine and synthesize random materials to make entirely new objects with completely different functions. We can discover things about how the universe operates. God gave humans authority over every other living thing. He designed us to be able to manipulate, control, and understand our surroundings. But He also designed us to recognize that our surroundings were made by Him. God is opposed to those who try to deny Him credit for creating the universe, and yet somehow claim credit and glory for themselves, when all they have done is merely discover what He made.

When you boil it down, that is all science really is - simply the discovery of what already exists, what God arranged and set in place. We observe plants and animals to discover how they thrive. We discover the distances between the planets and the stars. We discover archaeological and fossilized remains. We discover ancient scrolls and artifacts that help us learn what happened years ago. We discover gravity and how it works. We discover new galaxies. No scientist or historian creates these things, they simply discover them, and slap their own name on them, taking credit as if finding something makes it theirs.

Then, everyone comes up with their best theories about the implications of these discoveries, based on their particular area of expertise and experience. Quite often, scientists or historians in different fields will disagree with one another, or have multiple guesses as to what the discoveries indicate. They have many conflicting theories, such as what purposes old tools were used for, how the pyramids were made, or what happened to the Roanoke Colony. They bring their own human biases with them when they interpret the findings. We need to stop being afraid of science, and start learning more about the discoveries that provide evidence of the truth of the Bible, so we can share those with others.

The enemy has lied to the world about the validity of science. Scientists are humans like the rest of us. There is nothing special about their opinions, they merely observe the behavior of objects or living things, or set up experiments to manipulate and test their behavior. They then form opinions and assumptions based on how those objects behave. They make a lot of mistakes, because, like every human, they bring their own flaws and frameworks with them. These biases influence their ideas about the reasons for what they observe. This is what leads to arguments with other scientists, or people from differing disciplines, whose backgrounds might lead them to form a conflicting view. In the end, their assumptions usually turn out to be incorrect, and we once again have to update the science and history textbooks to match the latest 'facts'.

Despite knowing that science eventually almost always proves itself wrong, people still tend to elevate scientists to some sort of pedestal of perfection. It makes no logical sense to implicitly trust any scientist. Scientists are not above the temptations of power, greed, or prestige; they are just like the rest of us. We should always feel comfortable questioning their findings, or the assumptions that lead to their conclusions. There are almost always scientists who disagree with the results of other scientists. Rarely is anything ever conclusively proven, yet the media will report scientific hypotheses and findings as if they are indisputable fact.

Science only conflicts with God if you force it to. If you look at scientific discovery from the viewpoint that God created everything, and compare what the Bible says, to what science has figured out so far, you will see that many times, they match up. Where they do not match, science usually doesn't have much evidence. When you start to investigate these unproven theories, which the world generally accepts as true, you find that a) they can be reconciled with the Bible, or b) the science we rely on is not as solid as we have been led to believe. In fact, if you read scientific articles and studies, you will see that they use words like 'believe' and 'assume' just as much, if not more, than Christians.

For example, God said, 'Light: be!' and light was. Which sounds a lot like what science describes as the Big Bang Theory. God spoke, and light banged into existence. God spoke, and the stars and the moon all banged into existence. And so on. Another big conflict has to do with the age of the Earth. The Old Earth Theory really does not make much sense. People are convinced that the Earth has existed for billions of years, even though scientists admit their belief in its age is an estimate, which means this is unproven. The problem for scientists is they have no way to verify this claim. We have absolutely no way of knowing how any elements behave over a million years, because we have never been able to observe them for that long. Scientists tell us that the earth is always churning. This means things that supposedly existed, and were buried, millions of years ago, are now somehow close enough to the surface that we can dig them out relatively easily. Scientists claim that this is a result of shifts and movement in the earth. Yet somehow all of these fossils survived these shifts and weren't pulverized into pieces or rotted away to nothing?

On the other hand, we are also told that the current theories of dating tell us that the fossils we dig up are millions of years old. The trouble with the methods we use for dating, is that there is no way to date objects like fossils. Scientists must take samples of the rock around the object, and then use various methods to determine a vast range for the age of the rock. They then make the assumption that the fossil that was encased in the rock is the same age as the rock itself.

But if the science is also correct that there is a rock cycle, and things are constantly being churned around in the earth, and that plates shift enough to make ocean floors into mountaintops, or move million-year-old dinosaur bones to the top of our crust, then how did all of these fossils survive the rock cycle for supposedly millions of years, some with tissue and blood cells still on them? Furthermore, how can we possibly know, with any certainty, if the rock we find the fossils in, is the same rock that the animal originally died in? We also have found rocks that carbon dating tells us are younger, encased inside older rock. Not to mention, if you send the same rock sample to three different labs, you will get three wildly different estimates of age.

Don't let anyone convince you that the science is settled on any of these matters. Currently, most of what you hear are just unproven theories based on erroneous assumptions. Try as they might, no one has ever proven the Bible false. Whenever someone tosses a scientific or historical 'fact' at you, investigate it. Do not fear it or concede its truth. Look into it. Is it actually a settled fact, or merely one of many theories? How much evidence do they have to support it? Does anyone disagree? Are there any exceptions to the rule? Is there a way to interpret the evidence in a way that fits the Bible? Does the evidence even actually conflict with the Bible? Most of the time, you'll find there is less evidence of their 'facts' than we have been led to believe.

One of our duties as children of God, is to have a response when someone attacks or questions the foundations of our faith. Not having a firm knowledge and understanding of Scripture, can put you in a dangerous place. Jesus had an answer from Scripture for every attack Satan threw at Him. He also knew our Father well, because He constantly spent time alone with Him. He was the Word made flesh. You have to be bold in your own relationship with God, and your knowledge of the Gospel. The Word is a powerful asset, it is crucial that we know it.

I have always been very argumentative, and I have always had a love/hate relationship with that part of my personality. On one hand, I felt like a smart, strong, independent woman. On the other hand, I felt like an angry, stubborn, know-it-all. My entire life, I had strong political and social opinions, and thought the other side were absolute blind morons. After essentially switching sides, and becoming convinced this new side was correct, I started to see how divided and deceptive the media had become. Most 'news' stations are heavily biased toward one side or another, and they all consistently leave out important information that supports the other side. Each side is only being fed information that confirms their own viewpoints, making the divide even greater.

As I expanded the news I watched and read, including international news coverage, I found out there was often quite a lot more happening beyond the slanted surface stories covered in the media. I realized so many issues I once thought were so simple, were actually far more complicated and nuanced. Both sides are being manipulated to keep us constantly arguing with one another, so we will ignore how they are using and taking advantage of all of us. They convince one side not to watch CNN, and the other side not to watch Fox News. They set up our newsfeeds and suggested videos to align with our same worldview. They deliberately work to reduce our exposure to the full story, so we grow even more divided. They know very few people will bother to seek out conflicting sources, or other forms of media, such as written articles, or international news. We are so lazy, we just click on whatever targeted videos pop up, or allow endless reels to scroll by. Our minds are easily manipulated, and we pass judgment on others at the drop of a hat.

Trying to share the Gospel in this already heated environment, with people who are firmly convinced of their beliefs, while also maintaining the integrity God requires, is a daunting and difficult task. I was terrified of God asking me to talk to people on the streets. I knew that if I stepped out unprepared and shaky in my faith, I would risk being pulled back under the devil's influence. This is one reason I preferred evangelizing in an online, written format, versus in person.

I knew the old me tended to get emotional and worked up when I argued about politics or other issues, and I was worried that would happen if I tried to talk about Christ. I did not know how to handle rejection. I worried I might not be able to compose myself well, or think quickly on my feet, should the other party become rude or confrontational. I was afraid I might accidentally say something wrong, as I frequently mix up names that sound similar, or start with the same letter. I once accidentally said Moses when I meant Mohammed, so I could absolutely make a real mess of things speaking out loud! By commenting in an online forum, I could wait until I was in a good frame of mind with the Lord, before reading a response. I could take a few extra moments to think about my reply, and I could more easily keep my emotions out of the discussion.

Nevertheless, my responses in online interactions are still very off-the cuff. I do not have a lot of free time, so I cannot spend hours researching and crafting my replies. I have included an appendix with QR codes and a link to some of the online conversations I have had with atheists, defending the faith. I thought of other things I could have said after the fact, but, as you will see, I am already very long-winded, so it is probably for the best that I didn't say everything! You will see all of my typos, mistakes, and language exactly the way I wrote them online, so I do not create a false expectation of perfection for people to aspire to.

I do not share them as some sort of outstanding example of how to respond to the various objections people have. I share them to show you what real-life, real-time engagement in defending the faith looks like. I may have missed a lot of points, but at least there was someone challenging the atheist worldview in that particular forum. If I had not responded, there may not have been anyone else in those threads who would have stepped up to the challenge. You will see that rarely did someone else jump into the conversation to support the push for a biblical worldview.

Some people might disagree with engaging in these online forums with atheists. I think they are wrong. In my opinion, it is exactly what God wants us to do, if we are able and called to do so. These answers get thousands of views. It is a field in need of workers. There are millions of people spreading misinformation and outright lies online; if no one steps up to be the voice of truth, how will we ever counteract these lies? We may find ourselves to be the sole person correcting the misinformation being spread. We must be brave. It is important that we have the ability to defend our faith against those who attack it. We cannot let the devil maintain his stronghold on the battleground of the media and social networks. If there is a field ripe for harvesting, we cannot refuse to work in it, merely because the plants have thorns. We have to put on our gardening gloves and get to work. We have to go where the unbelievers are, if we are going to win them over to God's side.

We are soldiers for Christ now, and we work on His side in this battle. The soul of each individual is at stake. They will perish because they do not know God, as we read in Scripture, "My people are destroyed for lack of knowledge..." (Hosea 4:6), and "For my people are foolish. They don't know me. They are foolish children, and they have no understanding. They are skillful in doing evil, but they don't know how to do good." (Jeremiah 4:22). We are fighting to reclaim souls alongside Christ, not trying to leave people in their unbelief, stuck in the enemy's territory.

It is our duty to help people. We must let everyone know that much of what they are reading from atheists and others, are lies about who God is. We must let them know the truth. Even if you simply start by correcting some of things being said, that can make folks curious. They may look up the verses for themselves, to see if what you just said is correct, and some might even start reading the Bible for themselves. This is how God expects us to show love to our neighbors.

Every soul of every person on Earth is worth saving. It is our job to share this Good News with all of them. But we know that this endeavor will not be easy. You will have to spend time figuring out the answers to their questions (and your own) in order to prepare. I included the examples of real-life interactions, so that you can see the types of questions and beliefs that people have, and then be prepared to respond to them yourself, should the need arise. Feel free to take my answers, refine them, and improve upon them, as you run into these questions yourself. Looking back, there are always things I could have said differently. I tried to always pray and seek the Holy Spirit to tell me what to write, so I cannot take any credit for any insightful comments. I am, of course, still human, so the mistakes are all mine. I am sure God will bless you with even more insightful thoughts to add.

You will notice one common theme, is that most people have never actually read the Bible, yet they all claim to know more than they do about it. Thus, many times their unbelief comes from a place of ignorance of the truth, not an outright rejection of it. The more I realized this, the more confidence it gave me to challenge their statements and beliefs. Since their opinions are based on shaky premises, they can be more malleable. This works both ways though. A belief in God that is founded on sand, will also blow away quickly when confronted or challenged. Ensure your foundation is solid before you step out, so it doesn't crumble when an atheist asks a particularly challenging question.

Very few unbelievers actually know and understand that you can talk with God, through the Holy Spirit, thanks to the sacrifice of Christ. No other religion says that every single human on Earth can hear their god(s). Some religious texts say their believers can talk to their gods, but none of them say they answer back, to anyone other than a random prophet. This is because they are not real; imaginary gods cannot talk to people. Most people, including most believers, have never read the Bible from cover to cover, yet they certainly have a lot of opinions, and make a lot of uninformed arguments, or excuses, for what they assume it says.

I recommend spending some time exploring the answers to some of the more common attacks on the faith. There are many books and other resources that tackle these issues as well. Once you familiarize yourself with common questions and objections, your own faith will be bolstered, and you will feel less shaky when spreading the News. If you still have a million questions yourself, it would be wise to spend a lot of time learning, before you throw yourself to the wolves. The disciples walked with, and learned from Jesus before they went out on their own. Knowing and understanding the Scriptures, and the evidence for our faith, is vital. Undertaking to research and share this information is a worthy endeavor. It is something every believer should do.

Another reason I share these examples is so you can see how you will be attacked for sharing your faith. People subconsciously feel judged when we share the Gospel. They have heard so much false information about who God is, that they assume the only possible outcome for them is condemnation. Because of these factors, people tend to lash out when others share the Gospel. To avoid feeling judged, they try to deflect, by pointing out the nasty behaviors of the people in the Bible, or they throw our own imperfection in our faces. They argue quite confidently about things they do not yet understand. It can be difficult to explain things to people who shout you down, or completely misinterpret everything the Bible says. It can feel impossible at times to break down their defense mechanisms, and get them to keep an open mind. Convincing them to forget everything they think they know about God, and start over with a clean slate, can seem like a lost cause.

There are ways to reduce the offense people will take at your sharing of the message. The first is to pray, before, during, and after. We must pray for the ability to speak boldly about God's Word, and yet maintain love and compassion for those still blinded by unbelief. You can pray for the ability to maintain your composure, speak peacefully, and avoid judgment and personal opinion. You can pray that you will be able to clarify their misunderstandings, while also being sympathetic to their strongly held convictions, because you remember what it was like to be held captive by Satan. Pray that their hearts and minds will be receptive to the message. Most importantly, you should always pray that the Holy Spirit writes or says the words for you.

Another way to reduce conflict is to stick to the topic. You should focus on responding to their legitimate questions with biblical teachings, and refrain from going back and forth on non-essential topics. No matter how tempting it might be to get drawn into side arguments about things like politics, this has little to nothing to do with God. Do not fall into the trap of becoming offended by their name-calling or ridicule, and whatever you do, make sure you do not hurl insults back at them. Remember they are blind and misled, they do not know any better, but you are fully conscious. You are at work, representing the kingdom, so be patient, even if you have to keep answering the same questions over and over again, like a teacher in a classroom full of kindergartners, or a server with a restaurant full of customers. Remember to hold tight to God's command to love your neighbor, as your guiding principle.

It can help to remember that you are not trying to prove anyone wrong, or win the argument. You are simply a messenger sharing information. It is as if you are a doctor warning your patient of the dangers of smoking. You cannot force him to stop smoking, you can only tell him what you know, and have seen. It is the same with faith in God. You cannot control whether or not someone believes the Bible. You cannot force faith upon anyone. They each have the free will to choose life or death, the same as we did.

Unfortunately, no matter how straightforward, calm, and loving you try to be, and no matter how Spirit-filled your words are, you have to know that someone will always find a problem with them. This is where the advice Jesus gave, to wipe off their rejection like we wipe the dust off our shoes, is powerful. In Luke 10:16, He lets us know that "Whoever listens to you listens to me, and whoever rejects you rejects me. Whoever rejects me rejects him who sent me." Furthermore, in 1 Samuel 8:7, the Lord says, "Listen to the voice of the people in all that they tell you; for they have not rejected you, but they have rejected me as the king over them." In other words, they have free will, you have explained the consequences of their choices, give them what they want.

Sometimes, it is best to just let the discussion go, pray for them, and wish them the best. Rather than go round and round in circles, or allow yourself to get drawn into wasting time with someone who is clearly only looking for a fight, you need to be prepared and willing to set boundaries. If you stay in communication with God, you will know when it is time to back off. Consider that your efforts were not in vain. With written or video forums, dozens, if not millions, of people might read or hear your comments one day. Something you wrote might plant a seed in some future reader's mind, even if they did not affect the original target.

You can never tell, the one who seems the most stubborn, might reflect on what you wrote or said, and begin investigating the idea of God more intentionally. Perhaps what you said did not convince them, but they will stumble across something that does persuade them, while they are attempting to find evidence to refute you. God always has a plan, and if He put you into place to write or speak those words, you can trust that they will land where He intends them to, even if you never know of their effect. It takes multiple exposures and experiences to learn any new thing. In the education world, we typically say it takes at least 14 quality interactions to learn a new vocabulary word, or five to seven years to learn a language, and that is for the average learner. Some people take longer. Learning about God and our salvation is no different. The information you provide, may not be what finally tips the scale, but at least you are adding one more weight to the side of Christ, one more exposure to the truth.

What if someone asks you a question that you do not know the answer to? First, rejoice! Thank God! Thank Him for the opportunity to learn something you don't already know. Thank Him that this new knowledge will help grow your faith to new heights! Next, pray about it, and ask Him for help to find and understand the answer. Then look into it. You can do this together if the person is right there with you. There is nothing you have to be afraid of, or ashamed of, in the Bible, so do not shy away from investigating the answers to their questions. There are many websites, books, and churches where people explain every word of the Bible. This is where knowing the Bible, and prayer, are helpful. You will want to compare multiple sources, and talk to God about what you are reading, to see if it fits with His Word.

In my experience, He has always guided me to the correct answer when I pray about it. As you research the answers to their questions, compare every commentary or opinion against what the Bible says. We have to know His Word well. Commit to finding out the answer for yourself. You will learn that, sometimes, God intends for us to use their objections and arguments, as signals for areas where we need to learn and be prepared. I have learned more about scientific and historical discoveries, as well as my own faith, simply because God has put people in my path who ask tough questions, and made me seek the answers. Rejoice in the personal growth these opportunities provide!

No matter what difficulties you face as you provide answers for your faith, you have to commit to not letting them stop you. Instead, research what the Bible actually says, and then, stick strictly to what you know to be true. If you are stressed out, or not in a positive frame of mind, wait to respond until you can center your focus through prayer. Silence is better than a frustrated or incorrect outburst.

Be careful out there, people are ruthless. Keep the Holy Spirit with you in every interaction. You have no idea who you are arguing with online. You could risk getting caught up in negative behavior, if you engage when you aren't prepared. These arguments and tactics could cause us to question our own faith, and highlight areas where we feel weak or uncertain. God wants us to deal with them now, by praying about, and researching whatever is troubling us, and not stopping until we get a satisfactory answer. It is impossible to know what random verse someone will throw in your face, or what objection someone will have once they find out you are Christian. But it will happen, all the time. You will be minding your own business, and a headline will pop up about '15 Bible Myths', or an ad on your social media for a scripture study program will lead to a comment section arguing that God is evil, and suddenly the Lord will compel you to respond.

Go out into the world, but be prepared. Don't be one of those 'people on the street' who gets tripped up when someone asks you a simple biblical question. I am not referring to random Bible trivia. I mean you must familiarize yourself with the common questions people ask about God. We have to be very careful that we do not fall into the trap of spouting off false information ourselves. If you do not know what the Bible says on a topic, it is perfectly fine to say that you don't know. Do not pretend or make something up, this would be lying, and we must be honest. We cannot simply repeat things we have heard our grandparents, random speakers, or the pastor on television say, because it could turn out to be very wrong, and thus add to the confusion that abounds in the world. Please personally investigate what the Bible does, and does not, say about the world. Would you go to work for any other employer, knowing absolutely nothing about your job? You must be diligent to know the truth, and the reason for your faith. You are a servant of the Lord Jesus Christ, it is time to act like one.

We have discussed that it is great to look in the Bible for answers to questions, but I do not want to neglect the importance of scripture memory when it comes to having a response to questions about your faith. I do not necessarily mean that you have to memorize scripture word for word. Rather, you need to internally know the lessons in the scriptures, and understand who God is, through your study. There may soon come a time when scripture memory will be more important than ever. If you found yourself thrown in prison for your faith, with no access to a Bible, do you hold it within your heart? We have to internalize scripture, in case one day we find ourselves unable to have a physical copy of the Bible. We may wind up passing the stories along orally, sharing what we each remember.

There is always a possibility that we could end up like other countries, where the Bible has been banned. We will have to know God's Word well enough to share it with others. You might also find yourself facing attacks from the enemy, but unable to access a Bible, or look on the internet at that moment. This is why it is so important to read His Word and pray daily, so you can have a solid relationship with the Lord, and have His words written on your heart. The more you know, the easier it will be to call upon Bible verses that will give your faith strength in a time of need.

Do not become discouraged if you feel intimidated, or if someone repeatedly fires off question after question, completely ignoring the answers you provided to their previous questions. God will help you with the answers, if you listen to the Holy Spirit. He may really want that information out there for a reason. As noted previously, perhaps the person asking the questions will never have a change of heart, but someone coming along months later might read your responses. Suddenly something clicks, and they understand. God always has a reason.

Remember when Moses was told to go and convince Pharaoh to let the Israelite slaves go? Moses was terrified to approach Pharaoh. He had previously fled because he was a murderer, and he had zero confidence in his speaking ability. He tried to object to God's orders: "Moses said to God, "Who am I, that I should go to Pharaoh, and that I should bring the children of Israel out of Egypt?" (Exodus 3:11), "Moses said to Yahweh, 'O Lord, I am not eloquent, neither before now, nor since you have spoken to your servant; for I am slow of speech, and of a slow tongue.'" (Exodus 4:10), and "Moses said, 'Oh, Lord, please send someone else.'" (Exodus 4:13).

Moses also worried about how he would respond to the inevitable questions, and that no one would believe him;

"Moses said to God, "Behold, when I come to the children of Israel, and tell them, 'The God of your fathers has sent me to you,' and they ask me, 'What is his name?' what should I tell them?". (Exodus 3:13), and "Moses answered, "But, behold, they will not believe me, nor listen to my voice; for they will say, 'Yahweh has not appeared to you.'" (Exodus 4:1).

Finally, Moses and his brother, Aaron, had to continually respond to and challenge Pharaoh. Over and over again, they performed signs and wonders, but Pharaoh refused to grant their request. This must have been incredibly frustrating and nerve-wracking for Moses. He did not want to have to talk to Pharaoh in the first place. Every time God worked some amazing miracle in Pharaoh's presence, I'm sure Moses must have thought, "This is it! This one will have to convince him!" Now imagine how he must have felt having to go back and try again each day, after the previous efforts were not successful. I wonder if he ever questioned God, or wanted to give up.

Of course, giving up would have been disobeying God's will. When we are in the moment, we are often blind, and do not realize God's actual purpose for the task. In this instance, it was not just about convincing Pharoah to let the Israelites go. We also learn that Yahweh deliberately hardened Pharaoh's heart, so that Yahweh could demonstrate His power over ten Egyptian false gods, one after another. After all, if He can turn the Nile river to blood, or multiply frogs, how could those things possibly be gods? What might have seemed like repeated failures to Moses and Aaron, were actually brilliant displays of Yahweh's power. So, instead of being annoyed or upset when your arguments are not working, rejoice when you encounter a particularly stubborn atheist. Perhaps God is deliberately drawing out the conversation, to slay as many objections as possible.

Perhaps He wants you to practice seeking and allowing the Holy Spirit to speak through you, trusting that He will give you the words to say. Yahweh reassured Moses in many ways. My personal favorite is Exodus 3:12, where "He said, 'Certainly I will be with you.'" It might sound simple, but that is all we need to remember. When we are worried we will say the wrong thing, or that the person we are talking with will ridicule us, we have to stop, and give those worries to God. He will always be with us, so long as we want Him to be. When He asks you to do something, don't even think about trying to do it, without asking Him to be right there with you.

When you rely on the Holy Spirit, you do not need to fear insults or arrogance. Be bold and confident in your faith! They are the ones who are blind and confused, our eyes have been opened, and we know the truth! Remember how confident David was when he encountered Goliath. The giant was challenging them to send one man from the Isrealites to come and fight him, the winner claiming victory for their side. Somewhat understandably, all of the men in Saul's army were terrified of stepping out to fight Goliath on their own.

David was a young boy. He had only come to the battlefront to bring his three oldest brothers a package from their father, and to hear news of the battle. When he learned about Goliath's challenge, and the lack of men willing to accept the challenge, he said, "What shall be done to the man who kills this Philistine and takes away the reproach from Israel? For who is this uncircumcised Philistine, that he should defy the armies of the living God?" (1 Samuel 17:26) Imagine the confidence it took for a young boy to be able to call out a giant, while standing in front of grown men, who were bigger and stronger than him! He made them all feel like cowards.

He explains exactly where his confidence comes from, both to King Saul in 1 Samuel 17:34-37, and in his exchange with Goliath in 1 Samuel 17:42-47:

> David said to Saul, "Your servant was keeping his father's sheep; and when a lion or a bear came and took a lamb out of the flock, I went out after him, struck him, and rescued it out of his mouth. When he arose against me, I caught him by his beard, struck him, and killed him. Your servant struck both the lion and the bear. This uncircumcised Philistine shall be as one of them, since he has defied the armies of the living God." David said, "Yahweh, who delivered me out of the paw of the lion and out of the paw of the bear, will deliver me out of the hand of this Philistine."
>
> ...
>
> When the Philistine looked around and saw David, he disdained him; for he was but a youth, and ruddy, and had a good looking face. The Philistine said to David, "Am I a dog, that you come to me with sticks?" The Philistine cursed David by his gods. The Philistine said to David, "Come to me, and I will give your flesh to the birds of the sky and to the animals of the field."
>
> Then David said to the Philistine, "You come to me with a sword, with a spear, and with a javelin; but I come to you in the name of Yahweh of Armies, the God of the armies of Israel, whom you have defied. Today, Yahweh

> will deliver you into my hand. I will strike you and take your head from off you. I will give the dead bodies of the army of the Philistines today to the birds of the sky and to the wild animals of the earth, that all the earth may know that there is a God in Israel, and that all this assembly may know that Yahweh doesn't save with sword and spear; for the battle is Yahweh's, and he will give you into our hand."

We must go into the world with this same confidence, faith, and trust in God. David's strength came from Yahweh. David learned to trust Yahweh in his trials and training, so he was confident that he could trust Yahweh in the test. All of the men of Saul's army were Israelites, so, theoretically, they all should have believed in, and followed, Yahweh. Why was young David the only one who had such confidence? Why was everyone else terrified of the giant? They gave the giant more power than he actually had, because he seemed so big and sure of his victory. He made the soldiers forget how big our God is. Is your god the real, living God?

If God is real, if He created the universe, if He made all of these things happen before, then certainly, He can do it again. David knew and understood this concept, because he had witnessed God's power time and again as a shepherd defending his flock. The soldiers might have thought they believed this. They probably proclaimed their faith to their families and friends back home. When push came to shove though, and their lives were on the line, only David acted on his faith. Only David trusted God enough to take a huge risk. Are you hiding with the rest of God's army, safe at church, or on your couch, silent about what He has done in your life? Too fearful to confront the giants, the people around you who deny Him? Our Father is bigger than every giant. Let your faith spur you to action, don't let fear keep you from your work.

We are often like those soldiers. We back down when our faith is insulted or challenged. We attribute more power to our problems, to strangers on the internet, or even to our families, than we do to God. God can stand up to any challenge. Just like Goliath, or the walls of Jericho, all of the obstacles that stand in your way will fall, if you walk in the confidence of God. You do not have to fear atheists, or scientific challenges.

We know we cannot trust what the world tells us. The only person, place, or thing we must trust and have confidence in, is God. He created this universe, and every single thing in it, so if He says something, we can be certain it is true. Like David, we can rest assured that we have nothing to fear. We can aim, and let the rock fly, trusting that God will make it hit its mark. So long as we know and understand the Word of God, and listen to the Holy Spirit, we will hit the target. It helps to remember that we are not defending ourselves, we are defending the faith.

The Lord is coming soon, and we are sounding the alarm. We are telling people that they need to prepare their souls, and explaining how to do so. When we are engaging with atheists, agnostics, and people who worship false gods, we are not trying to attack them, or get them to believe in us. We are simply warning them, letting them know, Jesus is coming soon.

He will throw the evil in this world into the pit of fire. If they continue to stay trapped in the world, loving and holding tight to its sinful temptations, they risk being thrown in as well. We can tell them how much God loves them, and wants to save them. We can tell them how we have experienced His mercy and forgiveness of the bad things we have done. We let them know that we pray for Him to help us stop doing those things that will keep us trapped in death. We share how He has changed our lives, and how they should hurry up and join us before it is too late.

Since it is the job of believers to share the truth with others, their lack of understanding is at least partially our fault. We have been quiet for too long, hiding in our churches, allowing those preaching false doctrine and false idols to be the loudest voices. Learn about your faith. Take the risk. Engage and challenge atheists in a respectful way. Pray for wisdom and self-control to respond to their concerns. It is perfectly legitimate for people to ask questions. They have not been able to trust what they hear for so long now, that they have become skeptical of everything. They have been trusting in the wrong things. We have to be ready with the true answer. We have to be willing to seek the Holy Spirit's guidance on our response. Watch and learn from the faithful, read and study, attend small group discipleship classes, figure out what works for you, and then get out there and share the Good News!

NOTES

6

Humble Yourself

In that hour the disciples came to Jesus, saying, "Who then is greatest in the Kingdom of Heaven?" Jesus called a little child to himself, and set him in the middle of them and said, "Most certainly I tell you, unless you turn and become as little children, you will in no way enter into the Kingdom of Heaven. Whoever therefore humbles himself as this little child is the greatest in the Kingdom of Heaven.

- Matthew 18:1-4

If you are part of a large, close-knit family and you come home for a big occasion, such as your brother's wedding, what is your role? You walk in to find a bustle of activity. Your whole family is in the middle of cooking, setting up tables, and decorating. What do you do as a family member? Do you sit down at the best table to relax, demanding your family serve you while you wait? Or do you ask what needs to be done, and get to work? The family or friends who are closest to the bride and groom typically jump in to help. When we are part of a loving family, we serve one another. We are brothers and sisters, all children of God. We are preparing for the Son's wedding feast. We must be willing to become servants, and jump in to start helping out the family, as we plan for Christ's return. As we saw, one way we can serve right now is by helping to deliver the invitations.

I have made the claim that judgment is one of the biggest problems facing the church, and now I claim that humility is one of the more difficult and rare attributes to find in humans, including those who proclaim themselves to be Christians. Our lack of humility likely causes many of the problems we have in life. Yet, a spirit of humility is one of the greatest attributes we receive, the more deeply we embrace Christ and the Holy Spirit. Humility helps us serve God and put His will above our own.

Hold on a moment. Didn't we just say how cool it was when David boldly stepped up to Goliath? Yes, absolutely. But David's boldness came from his faith in God, not his own strength. His power came from his complete, humble submission to Yahweh. David constantly gives all credit to God, making statements like, "God delivered me". We are called to be servants of our King, not to become gods ourselves. As we know, however, being humble is not something that usually comes naturally to us. We are encouraged to be the best, to strive for promotions and leadership positions, to seek out honor and awards for our work. As we read, even the disciples argued over who was better. Once we turn our lives over to Christ, we must give that all up. Our only goal should be to honor God's Word. Humbling ourselves means we must put ourselves, our needs, and our desires beneath God's, because He knows better.

Jesus himself came down as a servant, and yet He is the most important person to have walked this Earth. He is far more important than any king, president, or leader who will ever exist. What is funny, is that we, who are of so little importance, try to do everything we can to puff ourselves up. There are billions of humans on this planet right now, and billions more have died since life began. You are special to God, and to the people who know you. Why do you need to be special to the world? Why do you need to feel better, or have more than others? Why do you need complete strangers to think you are great? God does not tend to look for the people who are already tooting their own horn, or greatly desiring recognition. He looks for the humble, faithful people, steadfastly working hard and trusting in Him, without any desire for their own fame and fortune.

Things like fame, popularity, and power are neither permanent, nor universal. There have been plenty of times where I, or someone else, has been excited to go to a concert for a band or artist that we were big fans of, but that no one around us had heard of. I remember, as a young woman, being in tears because I was so thrilled to be at a show for a band most of my friends did not recognize. The most important or popular person in a school, club, group, workplace, or team is only known, and only has authority over, those people who choose to be there. We voluntarily subject ourselves to their leadership and authority by participating. Often, no one outside of that particular sphere of influence has any idea who they are.

We flounce around making ourselves, and other people, extremely important in our own little worlds and minds, but outside of that, we (and they) have no power or influence. While you might be thrilled to run into your favorite celebrity on the street, someone else is going to walk right past them, and not have any clue who they are. When I lived in Las Vegas, I would have unknowingly walked right past the actor John Ratzenberger. He is the voice of many popular movie characters, but was known to me then as Cliff Clavin on the TV show *Cheers*. If it weren't for my secretary excitedly pointing him out, and going up to say hello, I would never have noticed him. Even after becoming aware of who he was, it had no real effect on my life.

Your overbearing boss or coach only has the authority you give him or her, by continuing to show up to work or practice. Your boss has zero authority outside of the workplace. If she showed up at my house or workplace, she would be treated the same as everyone else, regardless of who she is in another circle. The clique of 'mean girls' who run the school, or the housewives of the neighborhood pool club, do not actually run anyone's life but their own. None of these people are actually as important as they appear to be.

Considering all of that, it makes absolutely no sense to allow someone like that to control your life. Stop giving them power. We must be careful not to turn other people into idols. If we look to celebrities, politicians, and influencers to teach us how to run our lives, we will end up miserable, always chasing after something more. Good music is beautiful and enjoyable, and volunteering at your child's school is fantastic, but we have to learn to stop putting people on pedestals, just because we have seen them on a screen, or because they have power in some random organization.

We talked about false idols in previous books, but fearing the judgment of the catty PTA moms, or slavishly following celebrities, puts you in a dangerous place. None of them has any true power, only the authority granted to them, of a limited scope, and over a certain domain. As Jesus said in Matthew 10:26-31:

> So do not fear them, for there is nothing concealed that will not be revealed, or hidden that will not be known. What I tell you in the darkness, tell in the light; and what you hear *whispered* in *your* ear, proclaim on the housetops. And do not be afraid of those who kill the body but are unable to kill the soul; but rather fear Him

> who is able to destroy both soul and body in hell. Are two sparrows not sold for an assarion? And *yet* not one of them will fall to the ground apart from your Father. But even the hairs of your head are all counted. So do not fear; you are more valuable than a great number of sparrows.

How much of your mental and physical energy are you dedicating to them? Are you going to be available to do whatever it takes to be a servant of God, if you are worried about the opinions of those people? Does their judgment and influence matter more to you than God's? Fear instead the One who has power over every domain for eternity. If Jesus were to come back tomorrow, are you ready? If you are ready, is your family? What about your friends? Will the time you spend striving to please, or be noticed by, a group of random people, assist you with the goal of preparing for eternity in relationship with God and Christ?

We must also be careful that we are not seeking roles like these as a means of elevating ourselves, or stroking our own ego. If you are striving for these earthly positions, try to understand why you are doing it. Why do you want to open yourself up to a leadership role, or position of influence? Do you want people to know your name? Do you want praise and glory? Do you want people to respect you? Do you want more power and authority? Do you want to be recognized as you walk down the street?

This line of questioning applies to both secular and spiritual roles. We can just as easily fall into temptation, in either arena. Do you boast and brag about all of the good works you do, or show off how spiritual you are? Do you want to be the head volunteer coordinator, the lead deacon at church, or run the youth programming? Do you want to become a famous singer or pastor? Or do you want to use your abilities and talents to spread God's message, giving Him glory?

Ask yourself, why do you feel the need to prove yourself better than someone else? Why do you spend money on the things you spend money on? What would be the first thing you would give up, if money suddenly became an issue? What expense could you most easily live without? How would you feel if your power, status, or health took a nosedive? What if tomorrow you found yourself terminated from your job, or homeless due to a house fire? Would the people you associate with still care for you if you lost everything? Do you feel the need to constantly climb the social and economic ladder?

One problem inherent in trying to keep up with, or surpass, 'the Joneses' is similar to that of wanting others to think we are important or special. We do not all see the same things as status symbols. Some people focus on designer brands of shoes, clothing, cars, handbags, etc., while others could care less about brands, but amass degrees, awards, and titles. The president of the environmental activist group who drives an e-bike, is unlikely to be impressed by the CEO of a major polluter in his new private jet, and vice-versa. There is nothing that inherently makes one person better than another. To many, living in a mansion, driving fancy cars, and jetting around the world is a lifestyle to strive for, and the people who achieve it should be admired for their hard work, and cunning business skills. To others, those who have mansions, and millions of dollars, are grotesque, like a dystopian novel where the wealthy party is eating lavishly, while other human beings lay, literally dying, in the streets. Let them eat cake?

Our motivations are not always monetary. Some of us live for the applause. Sometimes we desire recognition and admiration. Trophies and awards are great, but really, very few people are ever going to see them, and no one really cares to hear us brag and show off all of our trophies. They matter when we are at the awards show or banquet, when the crowd is cheering, or within our particular fan-base, but when the lights are off, and we go home, they just become another line on our resume, or one of a million posts on social media. Our families are even only momentarily impressed, and then it is onto the next big thing, the next award, trophy, or prize. When we grow older, our physical and mental abilities tend to naturally decline, and we cannot compete at the level we once did. Someone younger and better always comes along. All of these earthly rewards, like fame and fortune, are fleeting.

Even worse, if you do hit it big, people tend to cater to you, thus you end up becoming the served, rather than the servant. If you spend your life living for applause, it can make it difficult to humble yourself, and be a servant. When everyone is looking to you as a leader or icon, it can put you in a very precarious position. It is so important to do everything in the name of the Lord, rather than focus on our own recognition, or the awards we receive. If you have a leadership position, or are in the public eye, pray and ask God to fill you with humility.

Seek to exercise your authority according to His will, and lead by example. Give all glory to God, do not take credit for yourself.

God looks for people who are not shouting about how great they are. He is looking for those who are shouting to others about how great He is. Neither you, nor I, have the power to save anyone. As repeatedly said, it was only God sending Jesus to pay the price for the world's sin, that saved us from death. Each individual must make their own choice of whether or not to accept that sacrifice on their behalf. When we accept it, we become children of God. Our earthly identities and roles that we aspire for, do not, and could not, save us, so why do we put so much emphasis on those earthly identities?

We aren't Superman, we are the news reporters telling the story of how he rescued us, and saved Metropolis once again. We are the messengers, God is the Father, Christ is the Savior. We brought nothing to the table but our sins, and our eyewitness testimony of how He saved us. This is why we must be humble. We are merely telling other people about what He has done for us, we do not need awards that judge which ones of us shared His message the best. We just need to share it, in whatever way we can, with as many people as He calls us to. We need to serve whomever He gives us to serve, and trust that our service in His name will help nourish their faith. If we are wrapped up in trying to win awards, and conforming to this world, we start to sound an awful lot like the disciples arguing over who was best.

In John 19:11 (in part), Pilate tells Jesus he has the power to set Him free. Jesus responds, "You would have no power at all against me, unless it were given to you from above." Any time we find ourselves in positions that carry some power, we must remember to be humble. We must remember that it is only by the grace of God, that we are in that position of authority or power, and that He could remove us from that position at any time, as He did with King Saul when He replaced him with King David.

In Luke 22:25-27, Jesus tells us it is better to serve, by setting the example of being a servant Himself:

> The kings of the nations lord it over them, and those who have authority over them are called 'benefactors.' But not so with you. Rather, the one who is greater among you, let him become as the younger, and one who is governing, as one who serves. For who is greater, one who sits at the table, or one who serves? Isn't it he who sits at the table? But I am among you as one who serves.

If we focus on our power and position here on Earth, we gain nothing but temporary earthly treasures that will burn one day. But if we focus on telling others of God's power, and of their heavenly position as children of God, we will gain heavenly treasures.

Even if you have always been the low man on the totem pole, and have never held a position of authority, you may still need to work with the Holy Spirit on humility. Humbling yourself also means that you stop playing the victim. You are here to serve, not to be coddled or served. No human being owes you anything. You do not need to seek vengeance, demand respect, or allow negativity to control your life. Forgiveness was discussed at length in *Belief to Pursuit*, but it is important to briefly look at it in the context of humility.

Forgiveness and humbleness go hand in hand. One day, an advice column on social media caught my eye. A woman was asking for advice about her abusive ex-husband. As I read the comments, most of them were telling her to "never, ever forgive!", and it broke my heart. Forgiveness does not mean condoning behavior. It does not mean you have to live with someone who is abusing you. If you can ask God to help you find a path to forgiveness though, you might be astonished at the peace it will bring you.

Forgiveness helps you as much, or more, than the person you forgive. By not forgiving, you are holding onto the pain, instead of letting God handle it. Whatever behaviors we do not forgive in others, we risk being judged for ourselves. If I plan to stand up before God, and complain that someone lied to me or hurt me, I had better be prepared to face all of the accusations others could make about my own lies, and mean behavior. Being forgiving and humble helps us to stop wallowing, because we remove our own ego from the events, through prayer. We are asking God to change our hearts, and our feelings, about what happened.

Forgiveness also involves allowing God to decide their punishment, rather than keeping their sins on your shoulders. Think of it like when one of your children hurts their brother or sister, or when one student hits another student at school.

Most parents and teachers tell their children to walk away from the situation, and ask an adult for help, rather than taking revenge on their own. They know if the other child starts hitting back, the fight will escalate, and someone will be hurt. By allowing the teacher or parent to provide the consequence, the instigator can be dealt with in a more rational manner, and hopefully further conflict can be avoided. Fortunately for us, it is not our job to punish our fellow human beings for all of their sins. We can leave that job in our Father's hands, as we already have enough of our own sins to deal with.

True forgiveness comes from understanding that the people who hurt you are being manipulated by the same evil forces that once manipulated you. It is recognizing that those forces are still trying to manipulate you, and turn you away from God. One way they do this, is by getting you to seethe over all of the bad things people have done to you. God forgave your own evil acts, and it is only through the power of the Holy Spirit that you are able to resist the enemy. You would not be strong enough to resist on your own, just like the people who hurt you are not going to be strong enough without God. We need to give them grace while they are struggling with the enemy.

Being humble means we stop taking offense to everything in the first place. We don't take it personally when someone else cuts us off in traffic or conversation. We don't steal, or get upset at the people around us when we cannot afford to buy something, or when our order is wrong. We don't feel slighted when we are overlooked, or not invited to the party. For me, this was one of the most difficult facets of humility to learn. I used to let things that now seem so trivial, change and control my behavior and emotions. For instance, I could easily be reduced to angry, hurt tears because of the disrespect I felt at work.

As a traveling teacher, I worked in several buildings, but did not have my own classroom or office space in any of them. Because I was not assigned to a specific building, I was often overlooked in the beginning of the year planning process. This meant I was usually assigned to an empty conference room, or shared space, as an afterthought. That was annoying enough to me, as each building knew that I was coming, and would need a space to work, but they never figured me into their room assignments. I also had to carry almost everything with me, so I had to pack it up when I left each day, and unpack it at my next building in the morning.

On several occasions, after setting up all of my things and starting to work with my students, someone would pop their head in at the last minute to tell me they needed the room I was in, for a meeting. I would suddenly have to stop what I was doing, pack up all of my things, wander around searching for somewhere else I could work, and then lug everything to a temporary new space, unpack, and start over. I would rant and rave, questioning why it was necessary to use my room, or why no one mentioned it sooner. I was upset at the lost time with students, and the disrespect I was shown as a colleague. The more often it happened, the more upset I became, and I lost my cool way too many times.

I felt very justified and righteous in my offense. However, as I was reading the Bible, I discovered that if we are trying to be like Jesus, we must learn how to give up our own ego, and need for respect. We must find joy in our role of serving others. I knew I needed to be humble, and move whenever I was asked to move. If, by giving up the room, I would make someone else's work day a little better or easier, then I should be happy I got to be a part of that. We do not have to necessarily remain in a situation where people are treating us poorly, but we do have to control our response.

When Jesus was being accused, tried, convicted, beaten, and killed, He never once carried on about how He deserved to be treated better. He never told them to quit talking to Him like that, or to keep His name out of their mouths. He did not even curse the people who were being malicious or violent to Him. If He humbled Himself, what gives us any right to exalt ourselves? Why should we demand respect where He did not? We are but servants of the Lord, even if some of us are regarded as kings or queens on Earth. He asked for forgiveness of the people killing Him. Certainly I could forgive those who only mildly inconvenienced me.

In fact, more than forgiveness, we must be kind to those who seem to be our enemies. We should not take matters into our own hands, or seek to play their games. Proverbs 25:21-22 tells us, "If your enemy is hungry, give him food to eat. If he is thirsty, give him water to drink; for you will heap coals of fire on his head, and Yahweh will reward you." In Proverbs 15:1-4 we read, "A gentle answer turns away wrath, but a harsh word stirs up anger. The tongue of the wise commends knowledge, but the mouths of fools gush out folly. Yahweh's eyes are everywhere, keeping watch on the evil and the good. A gentle tongue is a tree of life, but deceit in it crushes the spirit." The oft-stated phrase 'kill 'em with kindness' has its roots in biblical philosophy. The kinder and more gentle you are to the people who insult and mock you, the more you are following Christ's lead, and the more powerful your example will be.

We are not fighting against the person who is committing the wrongdoing, we are fighting against the tempters of that person. The battle is with the actual spiritual enemies who seek to steal our souls from God. We must work to try to help our fellow human beings ignore worldly temptations, and the voice of the enemy, and turn to God instead. Without His help, we could not overcome those voices of darkness. Those who want to hurt us are still trapped in that darkness, so we must help them by sharing the light of God with them. The hope is that by seeing and experiencing the love of God reflected through us, they will turn away from evil, and become another worker in Christ's harvest. If not, we do not have to worry, because God will handle it.

Part of our difficulty with being offended instead of humble, stems from our misunderstanding of what love is. This confusion about how to love is a stumbling block for many, including myself. In Matthew 22:35-40, Jesus says the two greatest Commandments are to love:

> One of them, a lawyer, asked him a question, testing him. "Teacher, which is the greatest commandment in the law?" Jesus said to him, "'You shall love the Lord

> your God with all your heart, with all your soul, and with all your mind.' This is the first and great commandment. A second likewise is this, 'You shall love your neighbor as yourself.' The whole law and the prophets depend on these two commandments."

Love is a command. Love is not a feeling. Love is something we must do even if we do not feel any particular goodwill toward a person. For example, if you and someone you love, perhaps your parent, child, or spouse, get into an argument, and you get upset and storm off until you cool down, does this mean that you do not love each other while you are feeling angry? Being commanded to love people means that even when we are angry, even when we do not *feel* warm, fuzzy, loving emotions toward someone, we still treat them with dignity. We still come back to them, and apologize, forgive, and make up.

You would not disown your child, parent, or someone you love over an argument, would you? I was planning to say, 'of course not', but then I had the scary thought that maybe this is why so many families are breaking up. There seems to be a huge trend of people going 'no-contact'. I read so many stories of people disowning parents, children, or other family members, because of relatively minor seeming arguments. They make videos about their family disagreements, seeking sympathy and judgment from strangers, rather than working on their issues within their own family. Lately it seems like people are so quick to quit anytime something gets the slightest bit complicated or difficult. We don't seem to give each other grace any more. If we disagree about silly things like politics, we immediately cut people right out of our lives.

We have been conditioned to think that all disagreement is bad, and that only our own opinions count. Anyone who disagrees with 'our truth', or our firmly held opinions, is no longer welcome in our spaces. Over the years, the media has gradually stirred us up, giving us the idea that everyone should agree with, and serve us. We do this when we think we are the main character in the story. We do this when all we think about are our own needs, and not about what someone else might be going through. We have forgotten how to forgive, and move past even minor slights, let alone how to work through and forgive major offenses.

We are doing a terrible job of loving one another. Every family argues, everyone has problems. Arguments should not mean the end of a relationship. I could not possibly count the number of arguments I had with my parents, especially as a teenager. We, and all of our friends, were even spanked as children. We would never have thought of disowning our families, or going 'no contact' over that. If we had, we would have missed out on complex, but extremely supportive and loving family relationships. Parents need to set boundaries for their children to grow safely and responsibly. They have to teach their children how to behave. Children should be loved, taught, and taken care of by their parents. Spouses should honor their commitment to one another. This is not easy, and inevitably conflicts will arise. This takes a willingness to put your own needs and desires behind the needs of other people.

Your desire for respect has to take a backseat. This is extremely difficult because we have been taught, over and over again, that respect is of vital importance, and that disrespect is never to be tolerated. People go into rages over seemingly mild statements or actions, because they perceive them as disrespectful. Let me put it bluntly. We have to stop. No matter who you are, you have no right to demand anything from anyone. You are here to serve and help guide others. You are not the main character. You never will be the main character. You are a servant of the King, you are not the king yourself.

Earlier we read we must be kind to our enemies. Jesus takes it even further and tells us we must also love them. Loving even the people who hurt us is part of God's command. As Jesus tells us in Matthew 5:43-48:

> You have heard that it was said, 'You shall love your neighbor and hate your enemy.' But I tell you, love your enemies, bless those who curse you, do good to those who hate you, and pray for those who mistreat you and persecute you, that you may be children of your Father who is in heaven. For he makes his sun to rise on the evil and the good, and sends rain on the just and the unjust. For if you love those who love you, what reward do you have? Don't even the tax collectors do the same? If you only greet your friends, what more do you do than others? Don't even the tax collectors do the same? Therefore you shall be perfect, just as your Father in heaven is perfect.

This means that, from time to time, we have to love someone who is very difficult to love. We may have to love them even though we disagree with them, and argue sometimes.

This does not mean that we have to stay in a dangerous situation, but it does mean that we attempt to help our enemies, as well as our loved ones, and seek to understand where their anger stems from. It means we encourage them to seek help to deal with their own underlying trauma. It means we do not allow ourselves to commit sins of our own because we foster hatred and anger towards them, in our hearts. We have to pray for the ability to see the human behind the behavior. When we do, we might see the small child they once were, who experienced abuse themselves. We might find that the angry 'Karen' is just a stressed out mom having a terrible day, or the crotchety old man just lost his wife of 60 years. Perhaps that would help us see them as a sympathetic people, in need of some help, and a relationship with God, rather than as enemies to battle and overcome.

You can separate yourself from someone without being hateful, nasty, and vengeful in return. Part of loving people is controlling our response to their hurtful or inconsiderate actions. Nothing in this world is so important, that it is worth hurting another human being over, either physically, or with our words and behaviors. What does loving our enemy look like? If you love the person who hurt you or taunts you, you do not lash out at them, you pray for them. You pray that God will call them to Him, and help them. You pray that God will help you overcome your offense at their behavior, and teach you how to deal with it. You pray for forgiveness and healing for both of you.

You are a servant of God. God is the supreme authority, and He controls who is in positions of power on Earth. This includes giving authority to people to lead kingdoms and other organizations. Therefore, we are subject to those in authority. The only time we should disobey authority, is if a law requires blasphemy against God, or causes us to violate His commands. Humility includes being willing to work under anyone that Christ puts in authority over you. Sometimes this involves hard things that we might not want to do, or that we personally disagree with. Think about the examples of Joseph and Daniel, who became slaves put under the authority of rulers who were outside the faith.

Joseph was an upright boy, but he had a bit of a pride problem. God needed to cure this, in order for Joseph to be cleansed and prepared. He was already his dad's favorite son, and very spoiled. The family dynamic was a heated, dramatic mess (think *Sister Wives*), thus his older brothers were envious and hated him. Their envy and anger also needed to be cured. So when Joseph went to his brothers, bragging about his dream that they and their father would all bow down to him one day, that was the last straw. They initially plotted to kill him, but instead decided to sell their little brother to slave traders.

Joseph then spent the next part of his life in Egypt, first as a slave, and then unjustly imprisoned for a crime he didn't commit. The entire time, he worked to his best ability for his masters. God humbled Joseph, and Joseph endured in his faith. God also humbled the brothers, making them live with their guilt, and their father's anguish, in thinking that his son was dead. I would have to imagine their actions haunted some of them for years. No matter how angry I might have been at my siblings, I would never have sold them to slave traders! It also sounds like their plan backfired, as their father grew extremely protective over his second favorite son, in his grief over losing Joseph. As messy as this all was, it is apparently what it took for God to get Joseph and his family where they needed to be. God's plan not only enabled them to survive the famine, heal their family, and save many lives, but He also cleansed their souls of their pride, envy, and wrath, preparing them for eternity.

One way or another, if you are committed to serving the Lord, He will teach you humility. For starters, it is one of the gifts of the Spirit. When you embrace the Holy Spirit, this is one of the ways He changes you. He chips away at the pride within your heart, and replaces it with humility. The faster you embrace these lessons, and let go of your pride, the faster He can remove that weed from your soul, and the less painful it will be. You have to stop holding onto the roots of the weeds. Stop pulling them down, while the Holy Spirit is trying to pull them up and out!

Don't make Him have to cause thorns to grow, and bugs to attack your hands, in order for you to let go of the roots of your pride. Joseph had to be made a slave and prisoner, what will you require before you let go? God had to humble Joseph's heart so he would be a compassionate leader when the time came. God wanted him to have the maturity to heal the situation with his brothers, rather than take vengeance. The sooner you relax your grip, and let the Holy Spirit pull your ego, pride, and vanity out of your soul, the more space you will open up for Him to plant humility.

Daniel, on the other hand, appears blameless and innocent, truly humble and obedient to Yahweh. He was taken as a slave, but remained peaceful, yet firm in his conviction to obey God. He declined eating the unclean food of the empire, while still remaining sympathetic to the servant who had been put in charge of him. Whenever he interpreted dreams, he took no credit, but gave all glory and honor to God. He maintained an impeccable work ethic, and because of this, Daniel was given a position of authority. That of course upset some people, and they decided to bring him down. The only crime his enemies could accuse him of, was his faith in Yahweh, so that was what they did. When Daniel prayed to Yahweh, in flagrant violation of King Nebuchadnezzar's order, the punishment was death by man-eating lions.

I find it so inspiring that even unto death, Daniel remained at peace, confident in the Lord. He did not rebel, fight, or argue. He accepted the authority that Nebuchadnezzar had over him - the law was made, the consequences were clear. This is part of free will. We always have a choice, but every choice has consequences. Someone holding a gun to your head is still giving you the choice of whether to do what they say, or die. Daniel had the choice. He could have easily followed the law, and avoided the lion's den. However, this would have meant violating God's Commandment to have no other gods before Him. Instead, Joseph chose to peacefully violate the human law, by continuing in his daily routine of praying to Yahweh. He was willing to face whatever consequences came with that decision.

Notice he did not do anything different, like spit in Nebuchadnezzar's face, walk the streets in protest of the law, or gather an army to storm the castle. He did not deny the authority Nebuchadnezzar had over him in that moment. He simply prayed, as always, knowing that he would likely face death. His strength was in the Lord's protection, and his faith taught him that there was no reason to struggle and make his soul unclean. He did not have to stoop to their level, because of what they were doing to him. He didn't even struggle against the lions, he just fell asleep! Daniel's story is an example to us of having humility and peace, no matter the circumstances, and it clearly showcases the awesome power of God.

Both of their stories are lessons to us. We are not supposed to be worried about fighting or striving to change our awful circumstances. We should be learning from them, and drawing closer to God through them. They should be driving us to pray about them. We should not be demanding more respect or authority, or being disrespectful to those in authority over us. We should talk to God about our situation, and ask Him to help us grow from it, and be fortified by it. We need to place our trust in Him, and follow what He tells us. If He wants the laws or circumstances changed, He will change them. We do not have to put aside our faith and obedience to God in order to appease humans. We need to develop the heart and attitude of a servant, rather than a boss or ruler.

This was rough for me to learn. I often thought I knew more, or could do the job better than my superiors. I have been praying for God to help me be gracious and humble, and to do the work I am assigned to do, without secretly grumbling about it, or gossiping with others about what we would have done instead. I discovered that once we become servants of God, we are meant to do what we can to meet the needs of others, but we are only supposed to rely on God for all of our own needs. We must put everyone else above ourselves, and become the lowest servant. We should ask for nothing from our neighbor, but freely and happily give what we have to anyone in need. When we are lacking something, we know Who to turn to. He will tell us what to do, send us the help we need, or point us in the direction we need to take.

Though you may have paid your dues, and worked hard to get where you are, you would not have been able to do any of that unless God had given you that ability. The only reason you have anything that you have, including your intelligence, skills, work ethic, or authority is because they were given to you by God. At any point, He could take any of those things away from you. You could be involved in a car accident that paralyzes you, find out you have cancer, or suffer a traumatic brain injury, any of which could topple you from your position of power or financial stability. We must realize we are all potentially just a few seconds away from a completely different life. There is a reason for the expression, 'there but for the grace of God go I'. Be willing to admit that on your own, without God, you are powerless and ignorant. Everything you think you have here and now, is really an illusion, so fighting for it, and lording your good fortune over others, makes no sense. You would not have it unless God allowed you to have it. Recognize that you also have flaws and make mistakes, and be thankful that God has given you the skills that you have. Ask Him to direct how you should use them.

If you continually put your faith in other people first, for example, calling your husband when you get a flat tire, before (or instead of) praying to Yahweh, be careful. The help of other people is not as strong or permanent as God's help. The people you rely on could leave, give up, turn on you, or be taken away at any time. God never leaves. God may answer our prayers by sending us people who can help us, but He always needs to be our first call, not our last resort. No matter what, His solution will always be better than ours, even if we never realize it. It may turn out that He tells you to call your husband for help with the tire, but things will likely go much more smoothly if you pray about it first. Be willing to admit that the only way you will make it through the most difficult times, is with the power of the Almighty.

In 2 Chronicles 20:12-13, we see how King Jehosaphat and the people of Judah humbled themselves to seek God's help. The king called everyone together to pray to Yahweh when they faced an attack saying, "'Our God, will you not judge them? For we have no might against this great company that comes against us. We don't know what to do, but our eyes are on you.' All Judah stood before Yahweh, with their little ones, their wives, and their children." The king was afraid, the people were afraid. In their fear they turned to God and admitted their weakness. They were at a loss, and pleaded with God, telling Him they had no idea how to beat these great armies that had come to destroy them. They knew God has the reputation of being all powerful, so they did the wise thing, and looked to Him to deal with the problem. They did not rely on their own abilities, or seek help from other human beings, such as a neighboring country. They put it into God's hands.

Then God responded! The Holy Spirit sent word through a man named Jahaziel, saying:

> Don't be afraid, and don't be dismayed because of this great multitude; for the battle is not yours, but God's. Tomorrow, go down against them. Behold, they are coming up by the ascent of Ziz. You will find them at the end of the valley, before the wilderness of Jeruel. You will not need to fight this battle. Set yourselves, stand still, and see the salvation of Yahweh with you, O Judah and Jerusalem. Don't be afraid, nor be dismayed. Go out against them tomorrow, for Yahweh is with you. (2 Chronicles 20:15-17)

Yahweh told them they did not even have to lift a finger in the battle because they relied upon Him. Jahaziel, one man in the crowd, was brave enough to shout out this prophecy. Everyone had to believe that this was a real prophecy. They had to trust his prophecy well enough to seek no other help, and stand still before a great army. They had to obey what God said through Jahaziel. It can be scary to rely on God when we have to stand in front of an 'army' of our problems, and do absolutely nothing. Sometimes, waiting on God, and doing nothing, is the most difficult form of obedience. It can be hard to trust His voice telling us to wait on His solution. The more practice we get in trusting God, the easier it gets.

When we fully trust Him, and obey, we discover that there is nothing He cannot do. He does not need us to be strong and powerful, or fight our own battles. He needs us to become humble, submitting ourselves to Him, and calling on Him to meet our every last need. When we do so, he can manage the battle without even needing us to break a sweat. Going to others for help, or doing things our own way, may often seem to work, at least temporarily. Of course, if we are wise, we know that our best ideas will never work as well as seeking to know, and follow, God's plan.

I'll share a fun, personal example here, that demonstrates how little effort we have to put forth to allow God's plans to come to fruition. For several months, my husband had been feeling a distinct pull to bring copies of these books to a Christian concert, and give them to one of the artists. We would imagine handing the books to them on stage during their performance. As usual, I was nervous about this plan, worried that it would annoy the performers. Amazingly, it turned out that God would not require us to come up with our own plan to accomplish His will. We just had to sit back and let it happen.

We attended a two-day outdoor music festival, and signed up to attend a free workshop on the second morning. After staying out late the first night, we were tired. We were not as motivated to attend the workshop as we had been when we signed up, but we went anyway. It turned out to be very interesting, and, as a bonus, the hosts gave all of us free tickets to a meet and greet for one of my husband's favorite bands! At the meet and greet, we were able to talk with the band, and give them copies of the books. My husband was able to complete the task God had set before him. No crazy attempts to throw books onto the stage in the middle of a concert were required! We simply had to be present, and willing to go wherever He led us.

Humbling ourselves, and becoming servants to God may seem demeaning based on our societal standards. We think of being someone's servant as restrictive and unbearable. We are taught that respect is extremely important. We insist on being called by our titles, and we will fight to defend our name and reputation. However, when you finally do become fully submitted to God, and agree to put yourself last, it is the most freeing experience. The weight of this world is heavy. The problems that get thrown on us, and the problems we create for ourselves, can feel overwhelming. When you become God's faithful servant, suddenly you have a supernatural helper to guide you and support you while you work through them. He is the boss, the manager, the owner. You can direct all complaints straight through to Him to handle.

When I used to work at a local family-owned farm stand and greenhouse as a teenager, we would frequently get customers who would try to get a lower price. They would claim they had a special deal, but we knew they were lying. We would fight and argue with the customer about the price, until they called over the owner's son (and heir to the family business), and he would usually just smile, shrug, and tell us to go ahead and give it to them. While we loved working for the son and his family, and we were treated well, this could feel so infuriating. We were defending his business, and felt undermined and disrespected when the customer would grin at us smugly. It also felt like they were getting away with the 'crime' of taking advantage of these kind people.

Until one day it clicked, and I suddenly realized that the son was essentially the owner. He was in charge, and it was his money and business, or it would be eventually. I was simply a servant who helped get his products to the customer. Instead of getting myself, and the customer, worked up by arguing, I could shout out to the son and ask him first. It was a relief knowing that I could dump all of those disputes onto him, and not worry about his response.

In the same way, it is an empowering experience to be able to give all of your concerns and cares to the Father, and let Him deal with them. Often, you will find that a problem that once seemed impossible to solve, suddenly resolves itself in the most miraculous way, when you give it over to God to deal with. In addition to our problems, we must also remember to give to God our successes. Even Jesus always gave credit to the Father:

> But when it was now the middle of the feast, Jesus went up into the temple and taught. The Jews therefore marveled, saying, "How does this man know letters, having never been educated?" Jesus therefore answered them, "My teaching is not mine, but his who sent me. If anyone desires to do his will, he will know about the

> teaching, whether it is from God or if I am speaking from myself. He who speaks from himself seeks his own glory, but he who seeks the glory of him who sent him is true, and no unrighteousness is in him. (John 7:14-18)

All glory and honor belong to the Father. Everything we do is from Him, and for Him. When you begin to get used to removing yourself from the equation, and giving everything to God, you will experience living in true freedom, even while in the role of a servant.

Notes

7

DIRECT ORDERS

Come to me, all you who labor and are heavily burdened, and I will give you rest. Take my yoke upon you and learn from me, for I am gentle and humble in heart; and you will find rest for your souls. For my yoke is easy, and my burden is light.

- Matthew 10:28-30

Teach me to do your will, for you are my God. Your Spirit is good. Lead me in the land of uprightness."

- Psalm 143:10

"David said to Solomon his son, "Be strong and courageous, and do it. Don't be afraid, nor be dismayed, for Yahweh God, even my God, is with you. He will not fail you nor forsake you, until all the work for the service of Yahweh's house is finished."

- 1 Chronicles 28:20

It seems that a common experience, shortly after coming to Christ, is wondering about our 'calling' from God. Many believers dream of how they will do something grandiose, perhaps becoming a famous faith-leader. Some may worry they will not be called to do anything. Still others may be *hoping* they are not called to do anything, because they are afraid of what that might entail. This hyper-focus on a specific calling could lead us to miss hearing the still, small voice of God. Hearing the voice of God is not easy, because our flesh fights against us, and the voice of the world is loud. All of our distractions can drown out His voice.

Instead of searching or waiting for one big calling, we should work on having such a close, intimate prayer life with God, that it completely reframes how and why we pray. The closer we grow to Him, the more we realize that our prayers should evolve into a minute by minute walking with Him, rather than sporadic cries begging for help, or structured praises at church. Our prayers should grow to the point where we are always asking God, "OK, I did that, now what's next?" However, many of us worry that we are not worthy, or capable, of having that level of intimacy with God. We think we are insignificant, or do not have the type of skills He could use, or the ability to do a huge task. We have to keep our focus on Heaven, not on our shortcomings, or the enormity of the job.

One problem is that we tend to have very short memories when it comes to prior miracles. We forget the past help we have received from the Lord. An example of this can be found in 2 Chronicles. King Asa of Judah had previously sought Yahweh for help when he faced the million men in the Cushite army, with only 580,000 men of his own. Though they were outnumbered, Asa cried out to the Lord. Yahweh struck the Ethiopians, and the Ethiopians ran. Unfortunately, later, when Judah was being attacked by Israel's King Baasha, Asa seems to have completely forgotten how well going straight to Yahweh worked the last time. Instead of crying out to the Lord again, Asa turned to another king for help. We read in chapter 16:7-9:

> At that time Hanani the seer came to Asa king of Judah, and said to him, "Because you have relied on the king of Syria, and have not relied on Yahweh your God, therefore the army of the king of Syria has escaped out of your hand. Weren't the Ethiopians and the Lubim a huge army, with chariots and exceedingly many horsemen? Yet, because you relied on Yahweh, he delivered them into your hand. For Yahweh's eyes run back and forth throughout the whole earth, to show himself strong in the behalf of them whose heart is perfect toward him. You have done foolishly in this; for from now on you will have wars."

Another example of forgetting previous miracles, are the two instances where Jesus fed the multitudes, with only a few loaves of bread, and some small fish. The first is described in the Gospels, including Mark 6. In that event, Jesus took 5 loaves of bread and 2 fish, broke them, blessed them, and fed 5000 Jews, like a shepherd feeding His sheep on the side of the mountain. They then had 12 baskets of bread left over. You would think that this would have stuck around in their minds long enough for the disciples to remember it the next time.

However, in the second instance, even though they had previously witnessed Jesus feed 5000 people from 5 loaves of bread, the disciples seem to have forgotten all about it. The next time Jesus says He wants to feed the multitude that had gathered to hear Him, "The disciples said to him, 'Where could we get so many loaves in a deserted place as to satisfy so great a multitude?'" (Matthew 15:33). They were still worried about feeding the people, even though they had already experienced Christ's solution to this exact same problem. Jesus then proceeded to feed 4000 gentiles from 7 loaves of bread, and had 7 baskets of bread left over.

The first time I read those accounts, I will admit I judged the disciples a little bit. Obviously they had just recently witnessed Him feed more people with less, what would be the difference now? Of course, I was humbled the very next moment, when I realized how quickly, and often, I am guilty of forgetting His power. I understood that we all forget the Lord's power, and the power of the Holy Spirit living within us. We forget that while we may be weak, and unable to solve every problem, we do 'know a Guy'. Hopefully by now, we don't just know Him, but we love Him, and are devoted to Him. So I endeavored to learn from these stories in the Bible. I wanted to guard against forgetting God's power. I prayed to make sure that whenever I started to look elsewhere for help, or started to worry about something I could never handle on my own, I remembered to look to the Lord instead.

This is so important, because if we do not remember that we are to seek the Lord first and always, for the solution to every problem we face, we can easily be overtaken by fear. When this happens, it is so natural to fall right back into our old patterns, and seek out our traditional sources of comfort. King Asa, when he was confronted with another enemy, forgot how Yahweh had helped in the past. He was scared and, as most of us tend to do, he appealed to another human for help. God used Asa's forgetfulness and mistakes as an example to us, that our first call for help should always be to God. He will let us know what our next steps should be.

We have to remember all of the miracles God has worked for us in the past, big and small. Why do we always forget? I think it is because the goal of this world is to get us to rely on our own strength for everything. We are taught that we have to forge ahead and make our own way. We are told we must be independent and self-reliant. When we finally get to a point where we realize we aren't strong enough, and need help, we are told to rely on other human sources. We think we, and the people around us, have to be capable of handling the problems. For example, we are taught that we must use our willpower to overcome addictions.

This can work sometimes, for some people. They can quit their particular addiction cold turkey, and never look back, seemingly successfully defeating that demon. Unfortunately, what often happens is that we give up one addiction for another. We quit smoking, but calm our nerves with salty snacks instead. Or we quit looking at inappropriate websites, but take up drinking, or weightlifting to distract us. As mentioned in *Pursuit to Commitment*, my use of honey as a sugar substitute was problematic, and merely a shift in the type, or focus, of my addiction to sweets. Our willpower may be enough to break one addiction cycle, but we can unwittingly fall right into another. This reliance on other sources of comfort keeps us away from God, when He should be our addiction. He should be our crutch. He should be our sole source of comfort and help. We know that true change requires the help of the Holy Spirit. Yet society has taught us that if we cannot quit on our own, that is a weakness.

Instead of seeking God in our weakness, we forget because we get scared or overwhelmed. In stressful times, our thinking can become automatic, and we go for the most obvious, common source. We look for conventional, worldly ways of solving our problems. Just like the first thing the disciples thought of was going somewhere to purchase food, we tend to think of the human solution first. It makes sense, after all, since that is what we have done our whole lives, up until we met Christ. Habits are tough to break. We forget that God has a better way, perhaps because we still have difficulty fathoming that God really is in absolute control. It takes deliberate practice to call on God for help first, every time.

We are also lazy, and tend to look for the easy way out, but God's way usually does not appear to be easy upon first glance. We want some secret formula, technique, ritual, or wonder-drug to work as a cure for what ails us. We don't want to have to do anything that takes us out of our comfort zone. We have little interest in modifying our lifestyle and behavior to fit God's will. We prefer to modify God to match who we think

He should be, so our lives do not have to change. Just give us an easy prayer, and a ritual to memorize, and we can be on our way. But when it comes to direct orders, God doesn't do that. As discussed in the previous books, this is not a religion, it is a relationship. Each of us has different needs and skills. Thus, there will always be different ways people accomplish obedience.

As we noted, to obey God means that we take every single problem to the Lord directly, and do not attempt to solve them on our own. The next part is to obey His instructions, no matter how crazy they seem to us. There are rarely ever consistent ways of doing things in the Bible. There are no magic spells to learn. Noah built an ark. Ezekiel had to stand (or lay) and proclaim God's words at the city gates and temple. Samson wasn't allowed to cut his hair. The Israeliates had to eat their food daily, without saving it, during the Exodus, but Joseph stored food for the seven year famine. Naaman had to bathe in the Jordan river seven times to cure his leprosy, while other men simply had to have faith for theirs to be cured. Moses had to first strike a rock with his staff, but then the next time, he was only to speak to the rock, etc. God does this to show us that obedience to Him is not some magic spell we can memorize and perform on our own. We have to listen to Him. We have to seek His instructions directly from Him, in order to know exactly what He wants us to do. We have to pray and listen for His voice. It is His power doing all the work, we are just the vessel for Him to work through.

It is not the activity we have to do that matters. The specific things we are asked to do, are really more of a display of our dedication to obey the Lord, through a positive action on our part (e.g., raise the staff and the sea will be parted). The power to do miracles wasn't in Moses' arms, or his staff, it was from God. This is why all honor and glory go only to Him. God is always the one doing the miracle. The raising of the staff was proof of Moses's faith that God would perform a miracle when he did so. It also made the miracle physically evident for the Israelites who witnessed it, because it is less likely to be a coincidence if these things happen precisely when Moses performs some action. It was proof that he was hearing instruction from God. When He says proclaim this, or do that, obedient servants say it or do it, even though it might make them look crazy to unbelievers. And when they are obedient, He follows through with the miracle.

Sometimes, though, what He asks is not anything different or unusual. In fact, He might ask you to do something you have already tried before, without success. When He first called Simon Peter, he was working on his fishing nets, and Jesus made use of his boat to teach from. In Luke 5:4-6 we read:

> When he had finished speaking, he said to Simon, "Put out into the deep and let down your nets for a catch." Simon answered him, "Master, we worked all night and caught nothing; but at your word I will let down the net." When they had done this, they caught a great multitude of fish, and their net was breaking.

Simon Peter pointed out that they had been letting down their nets for a catch all night long, and it had not worked. It is a perfect example to us that we can trust Him when He tells us to try it one more time. Do not risk missing out on miracles, because you are unwilling to give the simple things another try. When He tells you to do something, even if it has not worked in the past, have faith enough to try it anyway, just like Simon Peter.

Faithful servants obey the Lord without question. We are shown an example of this concept with the centurion in Matthew 8:5-13.

> When he came into Capernaum, a centurion came to him, asking him for help, saying, "Lord, my servant lies in the house paralyzed, grievously tormented." Jesus said to him, "I will come and heal him." The centurion answered, "Lord, I'm not worthy for you to come under my roof. Just say the word, and my servant will be healed. For I am also a man under authority, having under myself soldiers. I tell this one, 'Go,' and he goes; and tell another, 'Come,' and he comes; and tell my servant, 'Do this,' and he does it." When Jesus heard it, he marveled and said to those who followed, "Most certainly I tell you, I haven't found so great a faith, not even in Israel. I tell you that many will come from the east and the west, and will sit down with Abraham, Isaac, and Jacob in the Kingdom of Heaven, but the children of the Kingdom will be thrown out into the outer darkness. There will be weeping and gnashing of teeth." Jesus said to the centurion, "Go your way. Let it be done for you as you have believed." His servant was healed in that hour.

The centurion had faith that Jesus did not actually have to go physically to his house and touch the servant to heal him. He knew that Jesus merely had to give the order for the servant to be healed, and it would be done on His word. Faithful servants obey their master immediately, whenever they are given a direct order. They do not try to weasel their way out of the job.

God is searching for people who love and obey Him, and He will show Himself strong for them! When you trust in God with all your heart, you know that He can do anything. When you realize that, you reach a point where you stop worrying about what He will ask you to do, and you simply do it. You become the servant who obeys immediately, at just a word. You also know that anything and everything He tells you to do, will work out exactly as He intends, even if it isn't what you originally imagined.

God wants people who will obey Him completely. Think of it like a spy movie. The kind where the spy has a communication device in his ear, and a partner on the outside relaying information to him. The outside partner typically has visual access to the building that the spy is in. She tells him when to hide, when to make a break for it, which hallway to go down, or when someone is coming. The spy has to listen carefully for his partner's directions, and follow them immediately and precisely, in order to complete his mission without being caught. He trusts that his partner isn't going to give him directions that will put him in harm's way. He is not going to go left if she tells him to go right. We must become like the spy, and focus just as closely on the voice of God, shared with us through the Holy Spirit. We are tasked to obey God's directives immediately. This is not because we are forced to, but because it is only by listening to His voice, and obeying His commands, that we will reach safety.

We cannot try to outsmart God, and figure things out for ourselves. We cannot reject His instructions when we think they do not make sense, because oftentimes they won't. We have to learn to relax, listen to His voice, and do whatever He tells us to do, even if it seems weird. In 2 Kings 5:10-14, when Naaman, the captain of the Syrian army, had leprosy, he sought a cure from the prophet Elisha. He was initially taken aback by what he was told to do:

> Elisha sent a messenger to him, saying, "Go and wash in the Jordan seven times, and your flesh shall come again to you, and you shall be clean." But Naaman was angry, and went away and said, "Behold, I thought, 'He will surely come out to me, and stand, and call on the name of Yahweh his God, and wave his hand over the place, and heal the leper.' Aren't Abanah and Pharpar, the rivers of Damascus, better than all the waters of Israel? Couldn't I wash in them and be clean?" So he turned and went away in a rage. His servants came near and spoke to him, and said, "My father, if the prophet had asked you do some great thing, wouldn't you have done it? How much rather then, when he says to you, 'Wash, and be clean'?" Then went he down and dipped himself seven times in the Jordan, according to the saying of the man of God; and his flesh was restored like the flesh of a little child, and he was clean.

Naaman was insulted by God's orders, and refused to listen at first, because they did not meet his expectations. The Jordan was a dirty river, how could that cleanse him? If God was really a God of miracles, why should he have to bathe in the filthy river? Why wouldn't Elisha just call on God to heal him, or at least make him do some more appropriate task to be cleansed?

When things do not happen the way we think they should, many people will use that as an excuse to not believe in God or miracles. They do not understand that, while God certainly could 'poof away' whatever ailments they have, He is looking for trust and obedience. He is not a magic genie, He is the Boss, the Father, the Master, and He decides how things are done, not us. If you pray and He tells you to go to a certain doctor, who then heals you, is that less of a miracle because it did not happen the way you thought it would? If he solves your money problems by sending you help wanted notices, instead of a winning lottery ticket, do you ignore His answer to your prayers? We must learn to trust and follow His commands, no matter how trivial or ridiculous they appear at first.

Obeying God's orders is not easy. We do not spend enough time thinking about the desperation of the people in the Bible stories. Imagine the feelings they must have had, the doubt, fear, and grief, the downright dread and coldness in the pit of their chest, the feeling of being crazy. We must humanize the stories of the Bible, and not think of the biblical figures as somehow different from normal people. What kind of faith must it have taken for them to do the things they did!

For decades, people were assuredly calling Noah a crazy crackpot for preparing for the end of the world, and mocking him for wasting his time building a huge boat. Doomsday prepper! While they spent their time eating, drinking, and partying, he had to keep working and obeying God. When told to bow down to an idol, or to cease praying to God, Daniel and his friends determined to remain obedient to God, even though it meant the death penalty. What would it feel like to be bound and led to the lion's den, or the fiery furnace? Prophets throughout the Bible had to oppose kings, and other people, to proclaim the Word of God. Obedience to God is never simple or easy. It always requires some risk, or bold action on our part.

I had my own risk-related moment of judgment recently. I had been feeling stuck, not sure what to do next with the books and other projects. I was just overall not feeling very inspired. I felt like I was letting my workload overwhelm my connection to God. I was praying for reassurance, some direction, or an answer as to why I felt so blocked. While I was relaxing one day, I suddenly had the same line repeating over and over again in my head, to the tune of music. It was as if I was stuck in some never-ending one line earworm, and to make it even crazier, I was pretty sure the lyrics were in Spanish. I know just enough Spanish to get by, but I had no idea what I was singing in my head. It did not sound like a song I had ever heard before. I even tried searching for songs containing the phrase, to no avail.

It drove me crazy until I finally had to try to translate the phrase. My basic Spanish knowledge helped me take my best attempt at pronunciation and spelling. The translator then recommended these phrases, which matched what I was hearing: "porque no me dan mas te riesgos" or "porque no toma mas te riesgos". Apparently they mean "because they don't give me any more risks" or, "because I don't take anymore risks", or "Why don't you take more risks?" No matter which translation you pick, the message was clear. I had been holding off on sending out some books, and reaching out to people who could help me with my Bible study. I was playing it safe, and had stopped taking risks. God is letting us know that it is time for me, and everyone who follows Him, to take risks and be bold in our faith.

God asks us to take these risks, these leaps of faith, by doing whatever He tells us to do. Would you be willing to force yourself to get up every day for one hundred years, to go to work building a giant boat? Most of us regularly struggle to even get up and go to work, or do our basic chores without grumbling. How much more difficult is it to keep your faith when people constantly ridicule, or even attack you, for your beliefs? Once you start working on the things God is calling you to work on, you will also open yourself up to more attacks as the enemy tries to stop you.This is why the foundation of our faith must be strong, and why our understanding must be firmly rooted.

Furthermore, you will usually not be told the entire plan when you first start out, or possibly ever, and you have to be OK with that. For example, Abraham went out not having any idea where he was going, or what he would do when he got there. He was just told to leave his home and start walking. He had to have faith in the vague promises God made him. He had to walk through some scary places along the way, without having the full knowledge of what God had planned for him. He had to learn trust. It took much longer than Abraham anticipated for God's promises to even start to come into fruition, so he also had to learn patience. If Abraham had refused to move when God called him, he might have missed becoming the father of nations.

As it is often said, faith is commitment before knowledge. You are sometimes going to have to follow what God is telling you, even though you do not have all the information about His ultimate plan. You have to come to terms with not knowing everything, just like our spy cannot see what his partner sees on the camera. He has to follow what she tells him to do, even if it seems to be contrary to what he can see from his viewpoint. Like the spy, you have to commit to God's plan, without having the full vision of how it will all come together. Pray for the ability to be available on God's terms. Follow His directions, and He will guide you to exactly where He wants you to be.

Sometimes, God's plans seem to ask us to do something that involves a great risk to our livelihood, reputation, or even our life. It can be terrifying to be called to do something that puts you into a difficult or dangerous situation. Esther found herself in such a spot. She had a tough life. Orphaned, and raised by her Uncle Mordecai, she grew up a minority under Persian rule. When the king got rid of Queen Vashti for disobedience, he held somewhat of a contest to find a new queen. Esther 'won'. Haman, a wicked man in the king's court, was infuriated with Mordecai. Seeking vengeance, he hatched a plan to bring about a genocide of the Jewish people.

One day, Mordecai told Esther that she was called by God. Her mission was to convince the king to stop Haman's evil plot. This doesn't sound like a big deal, until you realize that, even as the queen, she could not simply go and speak to the king whenever she wanted. Anyone showing their face in his court without his blessing could be put to death. By appearing there unannounced, she would be risking her life. It took her quite some time to work up the courage to obey. When she finally overcame her fear, and trusted that this was her role in God's plan, everything fell into place. The king extended his scepter to her, and invited her to ask anything from him. Eventually she revealed Haman's plot, and his evil was turned on his own head. He was hung on the same gallows he had built to slaughter the Jewish people. Her story, and others in the Bible, show us the importance of obeying God's will, even when we are afraid for our own life.

Esther could have given into her fear. She could have rejected God's command for her, and attempted to stay safe in the palace. She could have ignored the plight of her fellow Israelites, hoping that being queen would be enough to save her from Haman's genocide. Like all of us, she had the choice of whether or not to obey God's orders. Either way, God's plans will move ahead, with or without our help. If we choose not to obey a direct command, we will face the consequences, as Mordecai reminded Esther, "Don't think to yourself that you will escape in the king's house any more than all the Jews. For if you remain silent now, then relief and deliverance will come to the Jews from another place, but you and your father's house will perish. Who knows if you haven't come to the kingdom for such a time as this." (Esther 4:12-14)

When God calls you to do something that seems crazy or scary to you, remember people like Esther. Remember that it is far better to take the risk, and be obedient to God, than to try to hide from God because you are afraid of what He is asking you to do. God's plans always have your true best interests at heart. Even when it seems scary, you can trust that it will work out for the good in the end. He will ensure His will is done. His plans will always be accomplished, with or without your involvement. It is not smart to ask God what He wants us to do, then consider it, and decide if we will do it. We don't get a vote if we want to be obedient, and if we disobey Him, there will likely be consequences. It is far preferable to participate when asked, as you will only make your own situation worse if you ignore His voice. Remember the parable of the talents from chapter two, and what happened to the servant who hid his talent because he was afraid.

God's tasks always come with a risk to our status quo. He disrupts our lives, and He changes us, carefully crafting us into the people He originally designed us to be. You will have to go out on a limb, fully trusting that God is holding your hand to stop you from falling, even if the branch breaks. These books required me to take a lot of risks. I never enjoyed writing in school. My life was extremely busy. I was frazzled and believed

I had no time to take on such a project. I was afraid and felt unqualified to speak about the Bible. I was aware that writing some of the things I would have to write could impact my job as a public school teacher, given the political climate. I thought I did not have the extra money required to fund this project. I had no idea how to even get started. I had to spend so much time up front, researching the steps to writing and publishing a book.

Before I began writing, I was being told that I would have to speak to people about my faith. I was relatively new to the faith when God first asked me to talk about it publicly. I protested like Moses. I am a nobody. I was not some famous Bible expert. I was not an online influencer, or even a popular person in general. Who would want to hear what I had to say? I reasoned that if God allowed Moses to bring Aaron with him, maybe He would let my husband speak instead. God responded to my suggestion by taking away my husband's voice for a couple of weeks following a surgery. I will leave it to him to explain the lessons he learned from that experience, but suffice it to say, I got my message loud and clear. God was asking me to do this particular task, not my husband.

Since I was fearful of speaking, He had me start by writing a book. I attempted to negotiate that assignment too, perhaps I could just write a blog article or two instead of a whole book? He counter-offered by telling me to write a series of five books. I tried to go back to just one book, He had me write down all five titles. I even tried to argue with God as He gave me the titles for each book, thinking it should just be a four-book series instead of five. I crossed out the titles of two of the books, and tried to combine them into one. I had this idea of what I thought the books should be about, and I was trying to make them fit my idea, instead of obeying what God was telling me. Four books seemed more than sufficient to me. As you can see, this is book number four, and book number five is in the works.

Then, even though I was still terrified, He immediately set me up to practice speaking about the books and my faith, through interviews on a local Christian radio station. Clearly, my training as a lawyer did not prepare me for negotiating with God. Based on my utterly useless attempts, I would not recommend trying to negotiate with God when He asks you to do something.

Writing these books also required a sacrifice of time and money. I originally set out thinking God's plan was to bless my hard work with a lot of money, by making these books into best sellers! Of course, I had plans on how I was going to use all of that money to grow His kingdom. Through the experience of writing these books, I learned a huge truth - money is meaningless. If God wants me to do something that requires money, He will give me the money I need to make it happen. These books are not a money-making scheme, they are my way of having a long conversation about God, with people who might never otherwise read the Bible, or seek Him on their own.

Even though I had been freely giving out the books to some people, I was still harboring a desire for wealth or income. His plan to cure me of my fleshly desire for money, was for me to give out hundreds of copies to the prisons and in the community. I had to learn to freely give with my whole heart, as many copies as possible, to as many places and people as possible. Rather than making money, these books would require me to give up money, for the purpose of sharing God. The Holy Spirit has been working within me, removing the part of me that desires wealth and fame, and replacing it with a desire to reach lost souls.

I had to send copies out to strangers, as well as people I know well. At first, I was so shy and reluctant to tell people I had written a book, or to give out copies. I barely mentioned them to people, and shied away from questions about them. I was so worried people would judge my writing, or my faith, that I allowed my fear to stop me from putting these books to work, serving God's purpose. They were doing no good sitting unopened in a box in my house. They were like a talent, buried and hidden. My husband was a little more bold, and he gave them to a few people at work, or to random strangers when we were out. Fortunately, their reactions were generally positive, so that motivated me to begin giving them out to people myself. I pray all the time that God uses them to help reach people, and strengthen their faith. I have already been blessed to see some results, as people have told me that, after reading these books, they have started to read the Bible, or have at least started to get curious about what God says.

Earlier, I mentioned that sometimes God's direct orders come in the form of very strong compulsions. In Jeremiah

20:7-9, we read about the prophet's reluctance to continue to speak Yahweh's words to the people, because he consistently faced persecution and threats. Jeremiah was essentially a street preacher, and he was tired of going out, day after day, and being harassed by everyone passing by. Ultimately, the compulsion to speak became so powerful that Jeremiah could not resist:

> Yahweh, you have persuaded me, and I was persuaded. You are stronger than I, and have prevailed. I have become a laughingstock all day. Everyone mocks me. For as often as I speak, I cry out; I cry, "Violence and destruction!" because Yahweh's word has been made a reproach to me, and a derision, all day. If I say that I will not make mention of him, or speak any more in his name, then there is in my heart as it were a burning fire shut up in my bones. I am weary with holding it in. I can't.

When God gives me sudden inspiration, I found out that it is best to immediately start writing it down. If I do not, I will sometimes lose the idea as quickly as it came. It is such a strange phenomenon, because it does not work that way for me for other areas of inspiration. For example, if I am at work, and I come up with an idea, or think of something that I want to add to a project, I can easily remember it, until I have time later to write it down. When God gives me book ideas, however, I learned the hard way that I do not usually have the luxury of waiting to record them until a more convenient time. After a few instances of completely losing all recollection of the wonderful idea He just gave me, I realized He expected me to drop everything, and write. He was teaching me to see His words as the most important thing. Nothing was a more valuable use of my time than focusing on Him, and His directives, in that very instant.

There have been multiple times where I have been in the shower, washing dishes, or lazily sleeping in my bed, and He suddenly gives me a great idea. I now usually spend a moment trying to convince myself I will remember it until a more convenient time. I struggle for a moment, before giving in and saying, 'ok, ok, I'm doing it!'. Then I quickly lean out of the shower, or stop washing dishes, dry off my hands, and jot down a few notes to help me remember the idea. There have been times He has woken me up at two o'clock in the morning to write a thousand words.

In fact, as I type this sentence, it is 12:18 am on an extremely early Thursday morning, really still a continuation of the day before, since I have not been to sleep yet. I have been running around since about 6:45 am Wednesday, driving over 5 hours, going up and down stairs, and walking all over on my weaker knee. I was planning to play on my phone, and relax until the washing machine finished, so I could throw my laundry in the dryer, and pass out. I thought that after I woke up, I could spend most of the day writing, while the kids were in school. The day had been long enough, so I wanted to start with a fresh mind after some sleep. Instead, I felt the compulsion to write, NOW.

I prayed and told God that my mind and body are kind of tired, so if He actually wants me to do this now, instead of just waiting til morning, He was going to have to let me know what to say. I had no thoughts or ideas to add at the moment, and no desire, or much energy, to try to focus on this right now. I sat with my finger hovering - games or writing? It took me about thirty seconds, but my finger obviously landed on the book, and now here I am, writing in bed in the dark at almost 1:00 am. At first, I just kind of scrolled through some of my notes I had jotted down, to see if anything inspired me, and I found this one, "Having to lean out of the shower or when half asleep to jot down the inspiration He suddenly gives". I cut it to paste it into the appropriate chapter, and remembered that I had already started writing a few sentences about this topic. He then showed me that I was living out the experience right now, and that I should simply explain it in 'real time'. Clearly I have attempted to do so, and the strange thing is, I have more energy now, than I did when I started writing.

I have never once regretted obeying these strong compulsions. Had I chosen the games on my phone instead, I would not have been able to write these words, I would have felt guilty, and I would have known I was disobeying His will for me. Eventually, I would likely have given in and written anyway, but then it would have been even later, and I would have been even more tired. I always feel so much joy and excitement when I make the choice to listen to God, and follow the path He is urging me toward. It is so much easier to just do it, and not put it off until later. If it is something God really wants you to do, He will do everything He can to convince you to do it at some point anyway. For example, let's look at the case of Jonah. Most of you have heard that he was swallowed by a whale and survived, but the story involves a lesson that Jonah had to learn the hard way:

> Now Yahweh's word came to Jonah the son of Amittai, saying, "Arise, go to Nineveh, that great city, and preach against it, for their wickedness has come up before me." But Jonah rose up to flee to Tarshish from the presence of Yahweh. He went down to Joppa, and found a ship going to Tarshish; so he paid its fare, and went down into it, to go with them to Tarshish from the presence of Yahweh. (Jonah 1:1-3)

Jonah was told by Yahweh to go and warn the people of Nineveh that they needed to repent of their wickedness, and return to Him. Jonah was afraid. Instead of obeying God's direct order, he attempted to flee and resist, by getting on the next ship headed in the opposite direction. Putting ourselves in his shoes, it isn't hard to understand why. Imagine standing outside a casino, or strip club, preaching to the patrons of those businesses about repenting from their wickedness. I am guessing you would not get the most friendly reception, and would probably be thrown out very quickly. I certainly could not blame Jonah, as I try to make excuses for why I cannot do something as simple as sit in my warm, comfortable bed, and type a few words. I like to pretend I would always do whatever God asked me to do, but realistically, I know that is not the case. I pray that God heals my weakness and disobedience.

Jonah was being asked to share the news in dangerous territory. Nineveh was a place Jonah had zero interest in going. Walking around hostile, wicked territory, trying to convince atheists, or people who worship idols, that they have to stop doing all of those things, and repent to Yahweh, sounds intimidating, to say the least. They would have wanted him dead! Jonah is also reluctant to bring them to repentance, because they are so wicked. In his mind, they deserve to be destroyed.

Jonah's plan to flee from God's order did not work; God sent a storm to batter the ship he was on. Eventually, the crew learns that Jonah's disobedience is the cause of all of the chaos. They ask him what they can do to appease God, and stop the storm from sinking their ship, killing them all. He responds, "Take me up, and throw me into the sea. Then the sea will be calm for you; for I know that because of me this great storm is on you." (Jonah 1:12) Jonah knows that he disobeyed God, and he knows the only way to rectify things is to give himself up, since he is the reason for the storm. He is too afraid to trust God and jump off the boat himself though.

The crew tried to avoid what they assumed would be killing Jonah, but eventually there was no other choice. They asked God to hold them harmless from Jonah's death, and they threw him overboard. Immediately the storm ceased. When Jonah rejected God's order, instead of making things easier on himself, he made things dramatically more difficult. Instead of dealing with the idol-worshipers in Nineveh, Jonah was now sinking fast to the bottom of the ocean. Through Jonah's story, God is teaching us to obey right away, so we do not make things worse for ourselves.

Jonah got desperate, and cried out to Yahweh as he sank deeper, and deeper, into the darkness. God sent a big fish to rescue Jonah at the last second, as he was drowning. The fish swallowed Jonah, and carried him in his belly until they reached the shore of Nineveh, where he spit him out. That must have been insanely horrifying. What would it have felt like to live inside a fish for three days? Again, we see how initial disobedience only makes things harder. Preaching on the streets of Nineveh is scary, but being thrown off a boat into a stormy sea, nearly dying, being swallowed by a fish at the last moment, living inside the fish for three days, being thrown up by the fish, and then still having to preach on the streets of Nineveh sounds far worse. Don't add to your trials and discomfort, by trying to avoid God's orders. Try to learn from these examples, so you do the right thing the first time. Don't be the person who has to hit rock-bottom, and nearly die before you cry out to God and obey Him.

When you are feeling like you have been given a task that seems overwhelming or too difficult for you, remember the obedience of Jesus. He was on Earth, fully human. He experienced pain, fear, and sorrow. He was asked to trust God enough to walk willingly to His death, and bear the punishment for all of our sins. We see the ultimate example of how we must handle the tasks that deeply grieve us. Jesus, like all of us, did not want to suffer pain and torture. The Bible tells us of His anguish over His calling in Matthew 26:36-44:

> Then Jesus came with them to a place called Gethsemane, and said to his disciples, "Sit here, while I go there and pray." He took with him Peter and the two sons of Zebedee, and began to be sorrowful and severely troubled. Then Jesus said to them, "My soul is

> exceedingly sorrowful, even to death. Stay here and watch with me." He went forward a little, fell on his face, and prayed, saying, "My Father, if it is possible, let this cup pass away from me; nevertheless, not what I desire, but what you desire." He came to the disciples and found them sleeping, and said to Peter, "What, couldn't you watch with me for one hour? Watch and pray, that you don't enter into temptation. The spirit indeed is willing, but the flesh is weak." Again, a second time he went away and prayed, saying, "My Father, if this cup can't pass away from me unless I drink it, your desire be done." He came again and found them sleeping, for their eyes were heavy. He left them again, went away, and prayed a third time, saying the same words.

Though Jesus was greatly troubled, and His soul was exceedingly sorrowful, He knew that He must obey God's will, not His own human will. He asked if there was any other way, but He ultimately submitted to what God asked Him to do.

At this point, you should be waking up to the notion that there is nothing more important than doing what God wants you to do. Obedience to God is your job now. Everything else comes after that. If you have to choose between what God is telling you to do, and the opinions of your family, friends, occupation, or your own desires, you should always choose God. Even if it seems like a huge risk to do what He is asking. Even if you do not have all of the information. Even if you have no idea how, or if, it will ever work. Everything will pan out the way it is supposed to, if you just trust and obey Him. Work on your relationship with, and obedience to, the Lord like it is a full-time job. Treat obedience to God like it is your life, because that is exactly what it is.

NOTES

8

DISOBEDIENCE

"Who then is the faithful and wise servant, whom his lord has set over his household, to give them their food in due season? Blessed is that servant whom his lord finds doing so when he comes. Most certainly I tell you that he will set him over all that he has. But if that evil servant should say in his heart, 'My lord is delaying his coming,' and begins to beat his fellow servants, and eat and drink with the drunkards, the lord of that servant will come in a day when he doesn't expect it and in an hour when he doesn't know it, and will cut him in pieces and appoint his portion with the hypocrites. That is where the weeping and grinding of teeth will be."

- Matthew 24:45-51

If anyone among you thinks himself to be religious while he doesn't bridle his tongue, but deceives his heart, this man's religion is worthless. Pure religion and undefiled before our God and Father is this: to visit the fatherless and widows in their affliction, and to keep oneself unstained by the world.

- James 1:26-27

"Now in the morning, as he returned to the city, he was hungry. Seeing a fig tree by the road, he came to it and found nothing on it but leaves. He said to it, 'Let there be no fruit from you forever!' Immediately the fig tree withered away." (Matthew 21:18-19) In the introduction to this book, we thought about how the wind and sea were examples of perfect obedience to Jesus. Now, as we turn our attention to disobedience, we once again look to nature for an example. People often question why Jesus cursed the fig tree. It all started with a long day, and a hungry Jesus. He reached His hand into a fig tree, even though it was not the time yet for figs. He seemed to be fully expecting that the tree would obey, and provide Him what He wanted. But this time, nature, the fig tree, did not obey Him. Because of the disobedience of the fig tree, He cursed it to no longer bear fruit.

Why would He keep around a tree that would not obey Him? Billions of trees obey Him, and faithfully bear fruit. If you have an orchard, and one of the trees bears no fruit, you would likely remove it, and replace it with a tree that does. You take out the dead tree to make room for the living tree. In John 15:1-5 we read:

> I am the true vine, and my Father is the farmer. Every branch in me that doesn't bear fruit, he takes away. Every branch that bears fruit, he prunes, that it may bear more fruit. You are already pruned clean because of the word which I have spoken to you. Remain in me, and I in you. As the branch can't bear fruit by itself unless it remains in the vine, so neither can you, unless you remain in me. I am the vine. You are the branches.

> He who remains in me and I in him bears much fruit, for apart from me you can do nothing.

When God commands you to bear fruit, and you ignore His commands because the timing isn't right, or the circumstances aren't perfect for you, that is disobedience. The excuse that 'it was not the right season' does not fly with God. He makes the seasons, you have to do what He asks, on His time, not yours. If you are focused on yourself, and your own timing, and not the voice and orders of God, you might find yourself on the path to disobedience.

Think about the miracle of Peter walking on the water to meet Jesus in Matthew 14:25-33:

> In the fourth watch of the night, Jesus came to them, walking on the sea. When the disciples saw him walking on the sea, they were troubled, saying, "It's a ghost!" and they cried out for fear. But immediately Jesus spoke to them, saying, "Cheer up! It is I! Don't be afraid." Peter answered him and said, "Lord, if it is you, command me to come to you on the waters." He said, "Come!" Peter stepped down from the boat and walked on the waters to come to Jesus. But when he saw that the wind was strong, he was afraid, and beginning to sink, he cried out, saying, "Lord, save me!" Immediately Jesus stretched out his hand, took hold of him, and said to him, "You of little faith, why did you doubt?" When they got up into the boat, the wind ceased. Those who were in the boat came and worshiped him, saying, "You are truly the Son of God!"

When Jesus called Peter to come out of the boat, he could have made excuses about how dark and stormy it was, complained he did not know how to walk on water and would drown, or asked a million questions first. Had he done so, he might not have experienced the miracle of walking toward Jesus on the water, even if it was only for a few steps. As soon as Jesus said, "Come!", Peter stepped out. He took a huge risk to instantly obey Jesus.

Of course, as we read in Chapter 2, the moment we take our eyes off of Jesus, and turn to look at the waves, we sink into the darkness. Peter's experience shows us that we must always keep our focus in one place if we want to be able to see God's miracles reflected through ourselves. If we start to focus on the world, and all of the problems around us, we lose sight of Jesus and forget we are walking toward Him. We sink in the midst of our troubles.

Disobedience is willful. It is deliberately ignoring what God tells you to do. I am a chicken. I have disobeyed God. So I know what I am talking about, when I say disobeying the Lord feels awful. He gave me one particular test, very early on in my walk with Him, that still sits with me to remind me to obey. Here is my candid Bible study journal entry from that day:

> Well I messed up. As I was driving to work, I moved over to the left because someone was changing a tire on the side of the road. As I drove past I realized that it looked like a woman was out by herself changing her tire. God told me I needed to go back and at least be there with her so she wasn't alone. I should have listened to Him and gotten off at the next exit and gone back around to help her. But I justified my own reasoning in my head (I was late for work, going back would have made me at least 20 minutes later or more, I wasn't going to be any more capable of changing a tire or helping. All I would

> be doing is standing there and she would probably say no thanks anyway if I did go back etc etc) I did not listen to God and trust Him that being late for work would be OK, or that just being there would help her feel better, but instead I ignored His direction.
>
> I am so sorry and so disappointed that I had the opportunity to show that I am learning my lessons and I didn't trust in You fully. I pray that God You will help me to trust in You and what You are telling me to do, even when my mind is telling me to do something else. I pray that You will help me learn this lesson and help me to know when it is Your will and Your word, and to follow You without doubt and without question. I want to be free of these chains in my mind that are binding me to the worries and cares of this world, that the enemy has designed to distract me from You and Your commands. I want to be a strong warrior for You God and to show people Your love and do nothing but Your will. Please help me overcome my fears and worries and doubts. Please help me to only look to You when I make a mistake and not to listen to the voices that are telling me that my mistakes have made me unworthy of Your love, I want to know and do Your command God. I want to live for only You.

As you can see, I felt a very strong pull from God that day, and I ignored it. He told me to stop. I reasoned that it was too late, and I had already passed her. He told me to get off at the next exit, about a mile down the road. I reasoned I was late for work, it was dangerous, and I wouldn't be able to help. He told me to get off at the next exit, another 2 miles down the road, but I reasoned I was way too far now. I was solidly stuck on leaning on my own understanding. I was afraid. I was still so caught up in the day to day worries of this world. I was more concerned about being late for work, than I was about obeying God. I faltered. I failed.

But I also got back up again. This is why I share these stories. I want you to see the ups and downs we all face, in real-life, current situations. They may not be the exact same situations as those faced in biblical stories, but they teach similar lessons, like that of Peter, who denied knowing Jesus. When he realized what he had done, he could have chosen to believe that was the end for him, but instead he was remorseful. He repented to Jesus three times, once for each denial, and renewed his commitment to Him. In contrast, Judas sold Jesus out, but instead of attempting to repent and seek forgiveness, he killed himself. These examples teach us that our shortcomings and failures do not have to be the end of our relationship with God. We choose the next step. If we listen to the lies of the enemy that tell us that this time, this particular act, was so bad we are eternally doomed, then we condemn ourselves. On the other hand, if we realize the error of our ways, and repent, turning back to Yahweh, He forgives us.

I repented for my disobedience. I sought His mercy, grace, and forgiveness. I asked to be cleansed of my unwilling spirit, and to be filled with only the desire to listen to and serve God. I begged Him to take away my disobedience. I even said that I would rather face His judgment, than be given over to the world, like David in 2 Samuel 24:14. When Yahweh offered him the choice of consequences for his sins, "David said to God, "I am in distress. Let us fall now into Yahweh's hand, for his mercies are great. Let me not fall into man's hand." Humans can be unpredictable and merciless, but with Yahweh, you know that He is always just and merciful. Choosing the judgment of God, over the judgment of man, reminds me of attorneys hoping for specific judges to be assigned to their client's case. Some judges are fair and rational, while others have a different reputation. The right judge can make all the difference.

It is best to never disobey God in any manner, and I pray for you, that you will stay strong and obey Him. Should you however, find yourself in the unfortunate predicament of having 'messed up' like Peter, David, or I did, I would suggest immediately throwing yourself at the foot of the cross, seeking His mercy and forgiveness. God is fair, merciful, honest, and just. I cannot say the same for most humans.

As part of my atonement for my disobedience, I asked to be given another chance. I prayed for help to release my fears when He calls me to do something. Not long after, I was racing to the school to bring my daughter her forgotten ID for the homecoming dance. When I was a minute away from the school, I saw two girls walking the opposite direction, down the road in their fancy dresses. Immediately God said, 'Help them'.

I would have had to turn around, so I continued into the school parking lot, and promised that if they were still there when I went back, I would offer them a ride. It only took a moment to give my daughter her ID, so of course they were still there. I had my youngest daughter with me, and I showed them my teacher ID badge, and offered them a ride. They were two young girls, planning to walk over four miles home in their high heels and long gowns in the evening. I am so thankful that God gave me another chance, and the opportunity to help them get home safely.

I make many, many mistakes, and am one of the weakest people you will ever meet. I want to reassure you that mistakes that are humbly admitted and repented, are certainly forgiven. God is looking at your heart. He wants a relationship with you. The blood and body of Jesus have paid the penalty for your sins. Now you can treat your mistakes as the lessons they are, and not turn away and hide from God because of them. When you turn away from God, the only other available option is to turn toward wickedness. Don't hide all of your troubles in the darkness. It is safe to bring your mistakes, weaknesses, disobedience, and troubles into the light, so God can help you clean them up.

In the story above, I mentioned promising that I would help those girls if they were still there. I must warn you that you should avoid, or at least be extremely cautious about, making vows and promises. Guard your words carefully. Your curses and vows may be binding. They can be a form of false obedience. We make vows and promises because of the mistaken belief that we have to bargain and trade with God to be right in His sight. We get nervous when we make a mistake, and in our human way, we sometimes want to try to correct, and make up for what we have done, or we want to blame someone else, and punish them for our mistakes. When we are stuck in either of those mind-frames, we can go overboard, cursing others, or dramatically committing ourselves to do things that God did not require.

I hear stories all the time about people who vow to God that if He will save them, they will dedicate their life to Him, or perform some other task. Maybe you've said something along the lines of, "God, if you will just help me get this raise and pay off my debt, I promise I will go to church every Sunday, and tithe faithfully." Hopefully you kept such vows, but if not, it is likely time to rectify that, through repentance and obedience. There are also those promises we make, invoking things other than God, such as swearing 'on my mother's grave' or 'on my life'. Are those binding on us as well?

Jesus tells us, in Matthew 5:33-37:

> Again you have heard that it was said to the ancient ones, 'You shall not make false vows, but shall perform to the Lord your vows,' but I tell you, don't swear at all: neither by heaven, for it is the throne of God; nor by the earth, for it is the footstool of his feet; nor by Jerusalem, for it is the city of the great King. Neither shall you swear by your head, for you can't make one hair white or black. But let your 'Yes' be 'Yes' and your 'No' be 'No.' Whatever is more than these is of the evil one.

He makes it pretty clear that we must not swear or curse, whether we are invoking His name, or mere earthly things. He reminds us that we do not have the power to keep vows, since we do not know what God's plan is for tomorrow. Whenever we make vows, we are effectively speaking in His name. We are promising things we cannot promise, because He ultimately controls whether or not an event occurs. We must be careful of what we say, and mindful of how we use His name. It is dangerous to throw it around idly. When we make offhand comments, such as, "I swear to God....", we are playing with fire. We do not know what is going to happen next, and we could find ourselves committed to doing something we never intended to do.

As I read the Bible, I noticed there were times where a person would inadvertently curse someone for life, or make a vow that cost them dearly. When I first read these things, I found them confusing and awful. For instance, I questioned why God would make a vow with Jephthah in Judges 11 that resulted in him killing his only child. I soon realized, however, that these people were not asked to make these vows and curses by God. They chose to speak words that carried the power to change their lives, by making vows to God.

In the sad, cautionary tale of Jephthah and his daughter, Jephthah was about to go to war with the Ammonites. In Judges 11:30-31 he made a dreadful mistake, "Jephthah vowed a vow to Yahweh, and said, 'If you will indeed deliver the children of Ammon into my hand, then it shall be, that whatever comes out of the doors of my house to meet me when I return in peace from the children of Ammon, it shall be Yahweh's, and I will offer it up for a burnt offering.'" Notice that Jephthah makes this vow entirely on his own.

God did not ask Jephthah to make this vow, or to bargain for his life, this vow was made entirely of Jephthah's own volition. God will save you, according to His will, not because of some bargain you make. In order to understand why Jephthah would make such a vow, we should try to consider his state of mind. He was the outcast son of a prostitute. He was afraid, going up against an army. I can only imagine that in Jephthah's past experience a house cat, dog, or some other animal, was always the first to sense him coming home, and the first running out to greet him. He assumed it would be the same in the future, which is why he used words like 'whatever' and 'it'. Animal sacrifices were common in those days. He did what many of us have done, and spoke rashly in his fear, trying to bargain with God for his life, by offering up one of his animals to the Lord. Unfortunately, since he could not see the future, he wound up deeply regretting his vow.

God allowed Jephthah the victory in battle, and he kept his life. Unfortunately, we learn in Judges 11:34-35 that the rash vow he made did not turn out as planned:

> Jephthah came to Mizpah to his house; and behold, his daughter came out to meet him with tambourines and with dances. She was his only child. Besides her he had neither son nor daughter. When he saw her, he tore his clothes, and said, "Alas, my daughter! You have brought me very low, and you are one of those who trouble me; for I have opened my mouth to Yahweh, and I can't go back."

Jephthah and his daughter followed through with his vow, trusting Yahweh, even though it must have been excruciatingly painful. It can be difficult for people to understand how both of them could willingly keep Jephthah's promise. This story is one atheists often bring up to try to claim that God is a cruel monster, who makes people sacrifice their children to Him. They make nefarious assumptions about the biblical roles of men and women, instead of seeing this as a lesson about making rash vows. God did not ask Jephthah to sacrifice his daughter, or to make any vow at all. In fact, God frequently contrasts Himself with the false god Molech, and those who worshiped him by throwing their children into the fire. That is the problem with making vows when you don't know what the future holds. Jephthah's assumptions led to unexpected consequences.

When we try to bargain with crazy vows involving life and death, we may end up doing things God never intended. God did not make Jephthah's daughter run out first, but that is what happened. Jephthah did not have to make that vow to win the battle. We do not have to offer Him 'payment' for our prayers, other than our complete repentance and submission. Our words carry power, they can speak life and love, or they can speak death and wickedness. One thing I really must pray for, is the ability to pause, and think carefully, before I speak.

Our job is to be men and women of our word ('let your yes be your yes...'). Do not promise some future thing, because you do not know what might happen. If you say something, mean it, and follow through. That is all. God does not want your crazy promises, because they are from evil, and they usually lead to harsh consequences. Instead He wants your only vow to be to commit to Him, and to listen to the sound of His voice. Then just do whatever He tells you to do. Nothing less, nothing more. He will take care of any battle you face, if you merely call upon Him. There is nothing you can promise to Him that He could not just do on His own, if that was what He wanted. He is your God, not your little brother, and He wants your trust, not your cheap bribery. He does not give us help because of the little promises we think we can make. How powerful would He be if He could only do something because of our promise?

We may not realize it, but by making those curses and vows, we take the glory away from God, and attempt to put the power into our own hands. This is a dangerous plan, because we have no power to save ourselves. We devise our own tests of our faithfulness, thinking we know better than He does. What should Jephthah have done differently? Rather than making a vow, He should have called out to God, and asked for help in defeating his enemies. Then he should have trusted, waited, and listened to whatever God told him to do. Jesus tells us to do the same. We can always trust that God has the best plan for us. We can trust that when we need reassurance, we can call out to Him, and He will guide our steps. He will let us know if there are any vows we need to make, we do not have to come up with them on our own. Don't make foolish deals and promises, they are not necessary. Jesus has already saved you, now you can simply let the Holy Spirit work within you.

We must also remember that if we do not keep our eternal life in focus, death seems a lot more awful than it really is. We do not really die, we merely fall asleep to be called up when it is time. Jephthah offered his daughter up to the Lord, putting her into His hands, and they both trusted that she would ultimately be safe. Death on Earth is not the end of our lives. While we must cherish and preserve the life God has given us, and not waste it, we also know that death is not our final resting place. It loses some of its sting when we realize that eternity is real. We know the sacrifice is only temporary.

In addition to rash vows there are other types of false obedience. False obedience encompasses many things, but generally stems from a lack of knowledge and understanding of the Bible. One example is reading, and re-reading scripture obsessively, but never praying about it, or applying it to your life. Like the Pharisees, you could know the Bible better than anyone else in the country, but if your heart is not filled with the Holy Spirit, the Helper, your understanding will be surface-level. I was guilty of this at first, always seeing how the lessons applied to other people. When I finally began to focus on how the biblical lessons applied to my own life, God's power really began to work through me.

If you do not allow yourself to be changed from the inside, it could lead to false obedience. This could be in the form of harsh and abusive behavior, justified as enforcing the obedience of those around you. Beating or screaming at someone might scare them into changing some behaviors, but it does not change their beliefs, and does not give them faith. It also makes your soul unclean. You cannot force another person to obey God, because our obedience comes from within our hearts. While your abuse of another person might make them conform to your standards, neither of you would be following God. You, because abuse is not love. Them, because they are following your rules out of fear, not Yahweh's rules out of love for Him.

False obedience could simply be doing things your own way, without consulting God first. You might decide to start street preaching, or to create your own charity, thinking that you are obeying God. If God has not asked you to do that, or if you have not prayed and presented your ideas to God for approval, then you are just shooting in the dark. This is what happened to Saul when he took it upon himself to perform the sacrifice, instead of waiting for Samuel. This is what happened to Sarah and Abraham when they tried to handle problems on their own. When it seems to us that God is taking too long, we can start to panic, thinking that we must have to do something more, or different to bring it about. Unfortunately, sometimes what we think is the right thing to do, actually turns out to create more problems. Turn your panic into prayer and patience, and wait for the Lord to do what He said He will do.

False obedience can also involve doing the right thing for the wrong reasons. Fasting, evangelizing, and working hard can all be beneficial things. However, when I was fasting to lose weight and appease my vanity, when someone preaches on social media hoping to amass a huge following, when we are trying to build our own brand, or when we focus on the financial profits of our outreach, we are being disobedient to God. Even though it may look like we are doing good works and sharing the message, if our hearts are in the wrong place, our efforts are misguided.

Everything we do is supposed to glorify God, so there should be no thought of seeking glory or earthly benefits for ourselves. This is why humility is of vital importance. When we remain humble, we know that making money, and achieving personal fame are so trivial. We cannot take those things with us to eternity. If we give those things up to Him now, God will give us so much better later. There is no point in seeking earthly rewards that will burn when Christ returns. The desires of our hearts motivate our actions. It is your heart that determines whether you are just performing shallow 'good works' for the sake of showing off, or truly obeying God.

Our Spirit-given humility should replace our pride, and remove our desire for fame and fortune. Humility guards us against such temptation. When we are no longer tempted by these worldly things, the enemy loses some major weapons against us. Where is your heart? Is it with God and His eternal promises, or is it on the lure of what the world tells us to strive for? Are you performing to an earthly standard, or are you excitedly participating with God in the mission of saving souls? Who are you trying to please? Yourself? Other people? Or God? Do a heart check when you are promoting your works. What are you working for? If you discover that any part of you desires fame, power, or money, pray for God's help to remove those desires from your heart, so that you cannot be tempted by them any more. Pray for Him to make your motives pure.

One of the most common types of disobedience happens due to a lack of faith in God's plan, causing us to fear and doubt. This leads us to attempt our own human solution to the problems we are facing. We think we need to speed up what God has promised us, or we allow our fear to convince us that God is not enough to get us through. We see this in the case of Abraham and Sarah. Twice, as they traveled through hostile territory, Abraham lied about his relationship with Sarah, and forced his wife and others to commit adultery. He did this out of fear, believing that if they knew she was his wife, they would kill him and keep her. Then, as they got older and older, they assumed that God's promise of heirs for Abraham was never going to come true. In their impatience, they again took matters into their own hands, and forced Sarah's servant Haggai to be a surrogate.

God had to step in and clean up the mess Abraham created each time. God was sending them where He wanted them to go, and He told them of His plan to provide them a son. Had they prayed, trusted Yahweh, and asked for His guidance and help, things might have gone a little differently. It is highly likely they would have received Yahweh's blessing of Issac, without all of the added stress and complications they created for themselves along the way.

We also saw how things would have been less difficult for Jonah, had he simply obeyed God the first time. He promises that His way is always better, and will always work, if we simply trust Him. Pray about whatever you are planning, and seek His counsel before you proceed. Don't make a move without consulting with Him first. Stop leaning on your own understanding of what you should do in any given circumstance, and make calling on God your first step. Do you want to only be able to accomplish what you can do on your own, or do you want to witness what God can do through you?

Another problem is delayed, or slow, obedience. I could have easily pushed off writing these books until the kids were out of school, or I had more time, but God gave me a timeline, so I must stick to it. This means sometimes I am editing late into the night, when I have not yet met my quota for the day. Being obedient means we cannot procrastinate. We must stop putting off the things we know we need to do. If you are supposed to start a Bible study, take a little risk and start it. If you feel pulled to work with youth, sign up to support an organization or group. You volunteered to be a worker in God's harvest when you accepted Christ. If He has called you to do something, He will ultimately make you successful. Even though it might seem scary or difficult at first, just take the leap and try it! Don't take forty years to do what should take two weeks. Try to just do it. Obey Him the instant you hear His voice. Otherwise, the longer you keep putting it off, the more opportunities you leave for doubt and fear to creep in.

As you delay, you start to think about all of the things that could possibly go wrong. You make excuses that you don't have the time, or you have no space to hold a meeting. You will start to doubt your ability to do any of these tasks. You may face discouraging advice from people you discuss your calling with. Life will take over. You will get sidetracked, and forget to sign up for the committee, or you will make other plans. If you put off obeying God, you could risk neglecting His calling completely.

This is allowing false idols, the things of this world, to trump what God has asked you to do. Imagine for a moment that Noah had been lazy, and didn't start work on the boat. What if Moses had refused to go back to Egypt and confront Pharaoh, David fled from Goliath, or Esther chickened out and did not go before the King? Would their stories have been more like Saul's or Jonah's? There is nothing more important than following God. Any other path leads to death and destruction.

When God asks us to do something, He usually does not want us to wait a few years before we begin the work. Unless He has told you otherwise, when you feel a calling, the sooner you get started, the faster God can work through your efforts. As noted, I am on tight deadlines with these books. Even so, my frail humanity wins out quite often, so I procrastinate and get distracted. Nonetheless, I know He has given me these deadlines to meet, and so I have to constantly pray for His help to stay focused.

I have to force myself to keep working, even when I would rather be doing anything else. I could make excuses, pretending to be a perfectionist, going over and over the books and doing more and more research. I could put off writing or publishing them indefinitely. God does not usually force us to work. He just has a way of strongly encouraging us to get it done, and making us feel miserable when we have slacked off for too long. If I had initially delayed publishing these books, out of fear that other people might not think they were any good, I would be disobeying God to try to preserve my own reputation. Over time, I might have even allowed my anxieties to overpower God's calling, and neglected to write or publish them at all. When God says move, that means it is the perfect time to move, so do it right away!

Sometimes the people closest to us stand in the way of our obedience. This is why we are cautioned, "Don't be unequally yoked with unbelievers, for what fellowship do righteousness and iniquity have? Or what fellowship does light have with darkness?" (2 Corinthians 6:14) This verse is a warning not to partner with someone who does not yet know Christ, even if they appear to have good intentions. There may be someone close to you, such as a spouse, parent, child, or friend, who actively campaigns against your faith and obedience. Perhaps they make demands on your time, belittle what you are doing, accuse you of being 'holier-than-thou', or otherwise refuse to support you.

We are to share the Good News with unbelievers, but we are not to team up with them in discipleship, or any other assignments God gives us. It is not wise to turn to them when you are facing attacks. Instead, turn to God, and other faithful people, for guidance. If God has given you an assignment, seek other believers for support, rather than relying on a friend or family member who is not a believer yet. Their lack of faith may cause them to be preoccupied with worldly gain, and other concerns. It could be very easy for them to drag you down with their objections, or misunderstanding, of how God works. They will think only of human solutions, instead of what God says we must do. The enemy might use their relationship with you to get you to the point where you do not finish the task, or end up doing something different that what God originally asked.

Even when working with believers, you have to be careful that they do not interfere with your obedience. They may not fully understand the mission God has given you. They may try to talk you into doing something else instead, thinking they are being helpful. It can be drastically more difficult to resist the well-meaning advice of another believer, because you may be worried that they are also hearing from God. This can make you start to doubt what He told you to do. In 1 Kings 13, we read of this exact problem. A prophet of Yahweh had traveled to make a prophecy to the king. Yahweh had given him specific instructions for his journey. He was not to accept any food or drink, and he was to take a different route home. He obeyed these instructions when first tempted by the king:

> The king said to the man of God, "Come home with me and refresh yourself, and I will give you a reward." The man of God said to the king, "Even if you gave me half of your house, I would not go in with you, neither would I eat bread nor drink water in this place; for so was it commanded me by Yahweh's word, saying, 'You shall eat no bread, drink no water, and don't return by the way that you came.'" So he went another way, and didn't return by the way that he came to Bethel. (1 Kings 13:7-10)

Unfortunately, while he was traveling, a second prophet heard of what he had told the king. He rode out to meet the first prophet, and by claiming to hear instruction from Yahweh, he was able to get the first prophet to disobey the direct orders he had been given:

> He went after the man of God, and found him sitting under an oak. He said to him, "Are you the man of God

> who came from Judah?" He said, "I am." Then he said to him, "Come home with me and eat bread." He said, "I may not return with you, nor go in with you. I will not eat bread or drink water with you in this place. For it was said to me by Yahweh's word, 'You shall eat no bread or drink water there, and don't turn again to go by the way that you came.'" He said to him, "I also am a prophet as you are; and an angel spoke to me by Yahweh's word, saying, 'Bring him back with you into your house, that he may eat bread and drink water.'" He lied to him.
>
> So he went back with him, ate bread in his house, and drank water. As they sat at the table, Yahweh's word came to the prophet who brought him back; and he cried out to the man of God who came from Judah, saying, "Yahweh says, 'Because you have been disobedient to Yahweh's word, and have not kept the commandment which Yahweh your God commanded you, but came back, and have eaten bread and drank water in the place of which he said to you, "Eat no bread, and drink no water," your body will not come to the tomb of your fathers.'" (1 Kings 13:14-22)

I assume after much travel, the prophet was thirsty and hungry, so he was easily tempted. The second prophet was saying exactly what he wanted to hear. He disobeyed what Yahweh had directly ordered him, because of the lies of the other prophet, which led to his downfall. When there is any conflict, the only way to be safe is to pray about it. If all else fails, trust the last instruction you heard through the Holy Spirit. You can never go wrong by obeying what you know He has told you to do.

In Matthew 16:22-23, when Jesus was telling the disciples that He would have to be tortured and die soon, He faced well-meaning objections, "Peter took him aside and began to rebuke him, saying, "Far be it from you, Lord! This will never be done to you." But he turned and said to Peter, "Get behind me, Satan! You are a stumbling block to me, for you are not setting your mind on the things of God, but on the things of men." Though Jesus loves Peter, He had a very difficult task ahead. He was troubled by His assignment, and Peter's concern was only making it worse. He needed support, not objections, from those He was closest to. He had to rebuke the temptations of Satan that were coming through the sweet, concerned voice of Peter.

As we are repeatedly shown in the Bible, God's tasks are not usually simple and easy. It takes perseverance and faith to follow through. The people around us may not understand what God has asked of us. To them, telling us to take some time off, or to avoid a dangerous task, might seem helpful. You have to ensure that you do not take their advice over God's directives. Refuting the objections of other believers, and the advice of those we love can be difficult, but if they are preventing us from obeying God, we must rebuke them. Trust what Yahweh has told you to do, and do not let anyone talk you out of obeying.

In the end, all of this comes down to one ultimate goal of the enemy, and that is to get us to give up. To become so distracted, fearful, or lazy, that we keep putting our job off, and never finish the task. This is the ultimate disobedience. When we decide we are too unable, useless, or unworthy to obey what God has called us to do, our light dims. Do not allow the enemy to place your light under a basket, and prevent you from following Jesus. Shine bright, in the confidence that no matter who you are, where you came from, or what you have done in the past, right now you are a child of God. So long as you put all of your trust in Him, and put your life into His hands, everything will work out the way it was meant to. Even though you may face obstacles, including torture and death, as Jesus knows, God's plan is always victorious in the end

In my experience though, it is far more common for people to have questions centered around knowing what is, and is not, allowed in the Bible, than they do about disobedience of direct orders. They become very legalistic, asking about the acceptability of specific behaviors. People want to know exactly how much they can get away with before a behavior becomes sinful. Where does God draw the line? Some things are obviously off-limits. Murder, lying, stealing, jealousy, adultery, idolatry, and anything else explicitly mentioned in the Bible as being evil in God's eyes, are all things we should ask the Holy Spirit to cleanse from us.

But what about things that are not explicitly mentioned in the Bible as forbidden? People have had these same types of questions since Yahweh first gave His Commandments. After Jesus came, many asked if they were still required to follow all of the Jewish laws and customs. They argued about things like whether it was ok to purchase meat from vendors that may have been used in sacrifices to false idols. They also argued over whether any gentiles who converted had to be circumcised, or otherwise follow the traditional Jewish laws.

Some of them legitimately wanted to know what God requires, so they could live accordingly. Others asked the questions to try to challenge those who believed, to justify their own violations of the law, or to see how far they could push the boundaries. Nowadays, people have similar motives, and though the questions might have changed slightly with the times, the overall themes are the same. Are we allowed to drink alcohol or smoke? Are there rules about appropriate clothing? Can we play virtual reality games? Can we cuss? We even ask the same questions people asked back then about circumcision and head coverings.

The short answer is that anything that takes your mind away from God, and from walking in obedience to His will, is not acceptable. Thus, the more complex answer to most of these questions is: it depends. As we discussed earlier, God's miracles occur in so many different ways because He does not want us to think that we have any ability to save ourselves. He does not want us to learn some ritual to heal the blind, and then rely on that ritual to cure blindness, instead of relying on God each time. The miracles do not come from the ritual, they only happen because someone has enough faith to call upon Him to provide them. These are not magic spells. He doesn't want us thinking that if we complete a certain number of tasks, or say all the right words, we will be saved. Our own actions cannot save us. The only way we are saved is through His grace, mercy, and sacrifice, not because we learned every ritual, finished some heroic quest, or followed every rule perfectly.

In the same way, with things that fall into gray areas, there is not always a cut and dry answer. What may be a problem for one person, can be nothing at all to another. Someone who is heavily worried about name brand fashion, easily tempted by vanity, has a hoarding addiction, or has been selling themselves further into the slavery of debt, might not be able to spend a day out shopping with friends. Someone else who does not have those same weaknesses, and just needs an outfit for a wedding, would not have the same risk of temptation. One person might be able to have a glass or two of wine on occasion, while someone who has struggled with an addiction to alcohol cannot have even a sip.

Remembering that we, as believers, serve as examples to the rest of the world, is another important factor in determining whether any of these negotiable things are allowed. We must consider that our actions represent Christ, and people will judge the Bible based on how they see supposed Christians acting. We also have to keep in mind that our actions not only affect unbelievers, but they also impact newer believers.

When someone first comes to Jesus, they are not usually familiar with what this faith requires. They look to the 'elders' of their church, the leaders, and those members who have been around longer, as the example for how God expects us to act. People often form their beliefs about the Bible, and what it means to be a Christian, by watching the behavior of believers. This is why so many people have turned away from the faith completely. They watched people who claimed to follow God, and know the Bible, do and say horrible things. They end up throwing out the baby with the dirty bath water. They give up on God because of the actions of false believers.

It is our job to avoid being one of the reasons someone else gives up their faith, or discounts Christianity entirely. Many of the things people consider 'negotiables' involve things that might inadvertently mislead others in some way. For instance, material things may no longer have a hold on you. You may understand they mean nothing, but you probably have a lot of weaker people watching your example. They are learning from your actions, what God considers right and wrong, and what is important in this world. When we hand out extravagant, frivolous prizes, and tons of money, as a way of getting people excited to come to church, or when we have fancy awards shows for volunteers, artists, or performers, we have to be very careful. Giving good gifts to people can be a beautiful thing, but it can also have a dark side.

One risk is that we can make it seem as if God is good because He gives us a new iPad, a pair of Jordans, or a pile of cash. Instead, we should be teaching that those things are worthless, and that God is good because He forgives us, and saves us from the lure of those temptations. We should be helping people overcome the desire for flashy material things, not encouraging it. Is it even wise to support these corporations with our personal or church funds? If we accidentally confuse people because they see us giving out rewards of material wealth, they might seek us, or seek money, instead of seeking God first. We might see it as fun outreach, or as a way to recognize people who have made an impact, because we no longer place importance on money. Unfortunately, many of the people watching will see nothing but gifts and dollar signs. This can encourage them to continue to look to money, as if that is an answer to any of their problems.

Others may begin to feel envious or resentful. They may see it as an indication that they are not pleasing God, if they are not the one getting rich, or being blessed with free money. We can create situations that tempt people, which is not the function of the church. We know that envy and resentment can lead to anger, and even murder in some cases, like when Cain killed his own brother. Prizes are not inherently bad, but they should be kept to a minimum, carefully thought out, and prayed about. If you do decide to give out prizes, they should be used for a limited, specific purpose, and it should be stressed and explained that the prizes are not gods themselves.

I have heard of more than one story of people feeling extreme jealousy or sadness, as they watched other people win prizes. One story that broke my heart was when I was listening to the radio, and I heard a man talking about the thoughts he had as a young boy, somewhere in Africa, waiting to be sponsored. He was in a program run by a charitable Christian organization. The organization recruits donors to select an impoverished child to sponsor, based on the child's profile picture and description. People might pick someone with the same birthday as their own child, or with similar interests. Many look for the ones who have been waiting the longest without a sponsor. Sponsors send in a monthly donation and write letters back and forth with their child. They can even visit them, if they are willing to travel.

This sounded like such a wonderful idea, but when the man started talking about his own experiences in the program, and encouraging people to donate, something he said gave me pause. When he was young and in need, he would sit with the other kids each day, waiting to find out who had been chosen by a sponsor. As the workers would read off the names of the kids who had been sponsored that week, they would get so excited and feel special. Someone had chosen them! He was excited for his friends as their names were called. Time went on, and week after week went by, and he still did not have a sponsor. He started to question himself. He wondered if there was something wrong with him, that everyone else was being chosen, but he was not. Maybe he was too ugly, or his picture was not good enough. Maybe he did not sound smart enough in his description.

Now, I realize that through that trial, he was learning a lot about patience, faith, and his own ego and pride. However, I also realize it should be a lesson for all of us. Is it good and reasonable for us to turn our charitable work into a contest, game, or spectacle? What if the organization simply assigned a child to each sponsor, in the order that they signed up for the program? We have to be careful of the message we are sending, and be cautious that we do not turn God's work into a capital-focused business, or turn our charity into a marketing strategy.

This brings us to the subject of money. Clearly it takes money, or some sort of means, to accomplish spreading God's word. We must try to exist peacefully within the bounds of society, to the extent it does not require us to blaspheme. This means, we have to pay what we owe. We may have to pay for a permit to have a public meeting, or for an internet connection and device to reach people online, or for paper, pencils, and stamps to write letters. You need tools to build shelters and plant food. The basic needs of Jesus and His disciples were supported by some of the women who were with them, and others along the way, who donated money, food, and shelter.

None of them became wealthy from their endeavors, and they endured extreme conditions. Their supporters often sold everything they owned to donate it to the cause. No one got paid a salary, they simply had their shelter and needs taken care of. No one was even the tiniest bit concerned about their personal wealth, because they were counting on heavenly wealth instead. If you think about how Jesus spent His days, He prayed, He ate, He walked, He taught, He bathed, He slept. There isn't much else. He wasn't saving for a plot of land or a summer cottage.

If we are honestly going to take a page from Jesus and the disciples, then technically none of us needs to collect a salary from our discipleship or charitable work. Our needs will be met by God. This is another concern I, and many people, have with large charitable organizations. Greed can infiltrate even seemingly philanthropic spaces. This leaves a bad taste in the mouth of the public. We have discussed before that money should be looked at as a tool, not the end goal.

I did some research into the salaries of the people at the top of many Christian 'charities', and it led me to believe that their hearts might not all be in the right place. When salaries across the board are all over $300,000 a year, and some are over $500,000, that is a huge red flag. When you consider there are usually several highly paid people running each organization, and they all need offices and benefits, the expenses climb even higher. Thousands of people, often struggling to pay their own bills, making far, far below those salaries, send in their hard-earned money to these organizations. They think they are helping people who are in need. Yet, it appears the first several million off the top of our donations goes to pay for all of the salaries and expenses associated with the leaders of these organizations. We do not need a team of cut-throat CEO's and business people, in order to provide assistance to those in need. If God wants our organization to have money, He will provide it, without all of the complications.

We are shown images of people living in tin shanties surrounded by danger, but these leaders live in huge, comfortable homes in wealthy areas. There is truly no reason why anyone needs to live that lifestyle in the first place, while others have nothing. This dichotomy becomes a much bigger problem for 'Christian charities'. The rest of the world sees it as particularly outrageous when religion gets involved. It looks terrible to the outside world when the CEO of a Christian charity is paid five to ten times what the average US worker earns. This is especially true when the charity is designed to help people in abject poverty. They see nothing but a scam organization making money off of the naive people who donate. It is one thing for a king to be wealthy, and have plenty of food in good times, but it is difficult to justify when his subjects are starving to death. Only an evil king hoards the supplies, while the rest of his kingdom suffers.

What we cannot do is allow money to become sinful to us. We cannot turn money into the goal or preoccupation. We cannot become greedy, desiring more and more. Not once in the Bible does it mention Jesus asking anyone to give Him a quarterly report and accounting of their finances. You never hear Him tacking on a request for an offering to His mission trip fund after every sermon or healing. He isn't investing, or thinking up ideas to bring in big donors. He just assumes that whatever He needs will be taken care of, because He is in constant communication with His Father, and He knows what He needs.

The few times He does mention gifts of money, are when people are donating to the temple, and making their charitable offerings to God, not to His campaign. He also states that the laborer deserves his wages, and that we need to help the poor. Thus money, or gifts of food and shelter, as a way of trading for services, in and of itself is not sinful. It is our hearts that make these things into sinful objects. Our greed is the problem. We worry about not having enough, so we constantly try to justify our desire for more. We also worry about how the people we support will use the money, when our only concern should be to give whenever God tells us to give. He will direct what happens to the donation from there. The only people who seemed overly concerned about money, were the ones who had sinful desires surrounding it:

> Then Judas Iscariot, Simon's son, one of his disciples, who would betray him, said, "Why wasn't this ointment sold for three hundred denarii and given to the poor?" Now he said this, not because he cared for the poor, but because he was a thief, and having the money box, used to steal what was put into it. (John 12:4-6)

Put money in its proper place, and your questions surrounding it will disappear. Chasing after, and worrying about money are both sinful acts. Ask the Holy Spirit to help you if you struggle in this area, and pray for the CEO's, pastors, and others who struggle with it as well. Ninety-nine percent of us do!

Alcohol is another example of a negotiable that can often trip people up. We are cautioned to remain sober minded as we wait for Jesus to return. This, in general, means 'keep your wits about you', and stay focused on Christ. Alcohol and drugs can cloud our minds, and cause us to lose that focus. Having a glass of wine or two is not forbidden. We often point out that Noah planted a vineyard, and Jesus drank wine with the disciples. What we do not often point out is that one particular episode of Noah's drunkenness led to a huge falling out with one of his sons.

There are a few major concerns with alcohol that should be considered. One, is that people lose their inhibitions when they drink, and this could lead them down the path to breaking a commandment. Many adulterous or dangerous behaviors start off with someone having a little too much alcohol - literally flirting with danger. Addictions are easily formed; sometimes it only takes trying a drug once, for you to become heavily addicted. This leads us to look to substances for comfort instead of looking to God. There are also health and financial issues that should be considered when determining if it is ok for someone to have a drink. Furthermore, we must remember that people look to believers to see how they act. If a weaker believer, or an unbeliever, looks at everything you do as the litmus test for what is or is not allowed, what type of example are you setting? We have to be careful that we do not appear to others to be promoting drunkenness, or reliance on alcohol as stress relief.

This holds true for any problematic behavior. People, rightly or not, pay more attention to how you act, than what you say. When they see self-proclaimed Christians acting a certain way, they make judgments and form opinions about what God allows. This is why we should never hold ourselves up as a standard of perfect behavior. It is disobedience for us to require perfection from others, when we are not perfect ourselves. Instead of pretending to be perfect, we should set the example of how to behave when we make a mistake. I try to make it clear that what I write in these books is not me judging you, because I also have my ups and downs. Thankfully there are fewer 'downs' each day! Sometimes I have a rough moment, and slip back into my old self. If I do something I shouldn't, I have to repent. If my children or others are witnesses to my behavior, I now apologize to them and tell them why my behavior was wrong. I want them to actually learn from my mistakes, and see how we should handle them. Setting the example myself is far more powerful than the 'do as I say, not as I do' philosophy of leading others.

When you encounter a challenge, how do you handle it? Do you go to God first? Or do you cuss and swear? Do you get angry and yell? Do you break down and panic? Do you dissolve into a puddle and cry? What do the people around you see you do? Once you realize you did not go to God first, what do you do next? Do you repent, and ask Him for help? Excellent. But then, do you make sure that anyone who saw you act poorly, knows that you have realized your mistake, and repented? You should apologize to them for how you allowed your behavior to affect them. Then set the example of how to repent, and rely on God. This is how they will learn to respond in the future, when they inevitably mess up, and find themselves in a similarly challenging situation.

His tells us that we must come to Him like children, following His lead, on the path to eternal life. Our actions should not cause anyone else to be tripped up or suffer while they walk next to us on the path. Our leadership must not cause anyone else to stumble or lose their way. As Jesus said in Matthew 18:1-6 and 10-14:

> In that hour the disciples came to Jesus, saying, "Who then is greatest in the Kingdom of Heaven?" Jesus called a little child to himself, and set him in the middle of them and said, "Most certainly I tell you, unless you turn and become as little children, you will in no way enter into the Kingdom of Heaven. Whoever therefore humbles himself as this little child is the greatest in the Kingdom of Heaven. Whoever receives one such little child in my name receives me, but whoever causes one of these little ones who believe in me to stumble, it would be better for him if a huge millstone were hung around his neck and that he were sunk in the depths of the sea."
>
> ...
>
> See that you don't despise one of these little ones, for I tell you that in heaven their angels always see the face of my Father who is in heaven. For the Son of Man came to save that which was lost. "What do you think? If a man has one hundred sheep, and one of them goes astray, doesn't he leave the ninety-nine, go to the mountains, and seek that which has gone astray? If he finds it, most certainly I tell you, he rejoices over it more than over the ninety-nine which have not gone astray. Even so it is not the will of your Father who is in heaven that one of these little ones should perish.

When you are filled with the Holy Spirit, you soon discover who you really are. You realize you are a child of the one true King, and that you are beneath no one else. At the same time, you also become humble, and realize that your fellow humans are children of the King as well. Thus, we are all equals. None of us should rule mercilessly over another, or think themselves superior, as we are all servants of God. To lead like Christ means to help lead others back to God, and back to life.

Just because we are walking in front of someone else on the path, does not make us any different, or better than anyone else on the path. We are all just rescued slaves being led out of captivity, and into freedom. We were taken by a warring prince, thrown in prison for our crimes, and forced into hard labor. But our King came to rescue us! We have to stay on the path, right behind Him, so we don't get lost again. Like Moses leading the Israelites out of Egypt, and Abraham pursuing his family's captors, we have to trust in our rescue, and follow the narrow path of our Leader.

Jesus showed us the Way, the Truth, and the Life, and we have to follow His lead. We have to do what He did. We have to give up absolutely everything for this one cause. We have to serve Him by helping Him gather up all of the lost sheep. Then we must continue to help by shepherding one another, as we trek along the path. This is done by reminding each other to call upon our Father, so He can fend off the lions, bears, and wolves trying to snatch us all up. We cannot join up with the enemy again, and become the predators of our fellow humans. We must love them, not push them away.

Your children, spouse, coworkers, and neighbors are all the property of God, the same as you are. He quite clearly states that murder, and harshness born of wrath are sinful behaviors. He does not want any one of His children being abused, or abusing His children. Our thoughts, words, and actions must always point to Jesus, and we have to remain vigilant that our behavior does not send the wrong message. Lead by example, by being a humble servant of God, by obeying His commands, and by loving and supporting your family and friends on their walk with God. Love is not negotiable, it is one of the most important commands God gave us.

Another form of disobedience is acquiescence to the evil in society. Consider if it is the best use of your valuable time and money to support institutions like Hollywood, the fashion and secular music industries, and others that exploit people. They often encourage everything that opposes God. There is a small, but thriving world of faith-based media you could transition to supporting instead. You could look for ways to cut the excess out of your life, and become more self-sufficient. Jesus gave up everything to spend all of His time walking with God, and sharing His Word. He left behind all of the comforts of this world, to save as many people as possible. "A scribe came and said to him, 'Teacher, I will follow you wherever you go.' Jesus said to him, 'The foxes have holes and the birds of the sky have nests, but the Son of Man has nowhere to lay his head.'" (Matthew 8:19-20). We have to be willing to give up everything ourselves, immersing ourselves in God, in His Word, and in helping others.

We can also acquiesce to the evils of society when we put up with false teachings or sin, especially within the leadership of the church. There may soon come a time when a government may force everyone to worship in a way that violates God's Commandments. If you acquiesce, you will commit blasphemy and idolatry. If you do not, you may face persecution and death. Most of us believe that we will be strong enough to resist, and that we will stay faithful to God in such a situation.

However, we are almost all currently guilty of standing by silently, while incorrect doctrine is being taught. Many of us attend churches that adhere to teachings that are not in the Bible. Then there are churches that will completely gloss over, or even celebrate, behaviors that God says are sinful. We hear the scandalous cases of priests who abuse their position and do atrocious things. What makes those cases even more horrifying, is finding out their behavior has been swept under the rug, and they were just transferred from place to place to avoid dealing with the problem. It is our job, within our community of believers, to hold one another accountable for upholding God's Word, in our teaching, and in our lives. This helps prevent someone coming to our particular church, and experiencing behaviors from the members that run contrary to biblical teachings, thereby causing them to turn away.

It is so difficult to counteract and correct all of the false doctrine, and false practices, that exist in the realm of Christianity. There are so many people out there teaching things, or believing things, that have nothing to do with what the Bible actually says. There are so many members of our local churches, including the pastors and their families, who are in need of admonishment and support when they continue to sin, or start to backslide. Unfortunately, we have been conditioned by society that it is rude to say anything corrective to anyone.

When I was younger, any parent or teacher could correct anyone's child if they saw them doing something wrong. The mantra was, 'it takes a village to raise a child'. If you saw two kids fighting, you stopped them, you didn't join in and cheer them on, or record them. Now, we are too afraid to question or say anything. The new rule has become 'mind your own business', even when it comes to being a witness to a crime. To me, this sounds a lot like Cain's callous response in Genesis 4:9, "Yahweh said to Cain, 'Where is Abel, your brother?' He said, 'I don't know. Am I my brother's keeper?'"

The answer to Cain's darkly sarcastic question is, yes, you are your brothers' (and sisters') keeper. As discussed in previous books, everything you do affects someone around you. One major problem when we dismissively say, 'mind your own business', is that people rarely do. Outwardly, we may walk away from a situation, or not react to someone's post or email, but as we are walking away, what are we usually thinking about? I am willing to bet that eight out of ten people discuss their thoughts on what happened, or ruminate on that topic for days afterward. We form harsh opinions of people based on what we saw, perhaps even discussing it with others later. We judge everything, and everyone, we see on any kind of media. Usually, we are genuinely happy for our loved ones, but we secretly gossip about those we are not as fond of. Truth be told, we tend to love being in other people's business.

When open, loving, and honest communication is discouraged, we allow problems to fester instead of being resolved. Instead of loving our neighbors, we end up falling into sin. Gossip and rumors creep in where love and honesty fall away. If minding our business means we fail to address issues, correct misinformation, or report a crime, then we are failing our family. We have to help each other find, and stay, on the narrow path. Sometimes that means having difficult conversations, and working through issues together.

The subject of admonishing the sins of others is a very tricky one, and it is difficult to do well. This element of biblical teaching seems to be very misapplied, or ignored entirely. Often, religious people will go around judging and condemning everyone else for their sins, without recognizing their own. We know we must help one another, and correct false doctrine, or bad behavior, but those can be delicate situations.

One of the foremost principles is that we must first be able to accept correction ourselves, before we can see clearly enough to help correct our brothers and sisters. It is a deal we make when we proclaim ourselves followers of Christ. We know nobody is perfect or above reproach, and that includes us. You and me. Without God, without Jesus, without the Holy Spirit, we would be nothing but wretched sinners ourselves. So instead of being offended when a brother or sister questions our behavior, we should examine our mind and heart. We should ask God to help us see and correct those areas of weakness. He will help us identify those circumstances that cause us to momentarily look away from the Lord, and disrupt our relationship with God. We should learn to keep a watch for our own personal triggers and temptations, and avoid them by praying immediately, whenever they strike.

When we suspect that one of us is struggling with a trial or temptation, it is our obligation to try to help them work through it, and get back on the path to God. We are not to judge them, or make them feel so alienated, that they walk away. Negotiables, or gray areas, can trip up believers and nonbelievers alike. Keep in mind the principle that we must make a distinction between a believer and a non-believer. There are two different ways to handle the sins of each.

The believer is the one we must admonish and correct. They have proclaimed themselves publicly as a Christian, and are holding themselves out to the world as an example of the kingdom of God. If they are not demonstrating fruits of the Spirit, or if you know of something inappropriate they are doing, it is your duty to calmly and privately help them overcome. You can help by reminding them of how to return their focus to Christ, who is walking ahead of them on the path to life. You can pray with them that they will be filled with God's guidance through the Holy Spirit.

Galatians 6:1 tells us, "Brothers, even if a man is caught in some fault, you who are spiritual must restore such a one in a spirit of gentleness, looking to yourself so that you also aren't tempted." In other words, help people, but be careful that they do not pull you down with them. When I took swimming lessons, we were always taught that if we saw a person drowning, we should throw a life preserver to them, and never jump into the water ourselves. It is not wise to jump into the water to try to rescue them, as in their panic, they can grab you and pull you under, causing both of you to drown. Be careful to remember that Christ is the life preserver, so keep Him as your focus, rather than trying to come up with your own rescue plan.

Basically, anything that is not explicitly dealt with in the Bible is best handled by having an open, frank discussion with the Lord, on a personal, case by case basis. Pray and ask Him what you must do. Look for similar examples in the Bible. Some questions to consider are: Does it affect your ability to focus on God? Does it get in the way of your practice of the spiritual disciplines? Does it become a false idol? Does it hinder your, or another's, obedience to God? Does it hurt the weaker brother, or encourage him to do something that violates God's commands? Has He directly ordered you to abstain from, or to do, something?

The answer to whether various negotiables are allowed often depends on how it affects you, and those around you. If, after praying, researching, and thinking through these questions, you still are not sure, why risk it? As the Bible makes clear, nothing you want to have or do on this Earth is more important than your relationship with God. The biggest question is, is it worth giving up eternity for?

Following Jesus can sometimes seem like being a character in an adventure movie. While trying to do the job God has called you to do, you might feel like you are trekking through the jungle, swatting back vines and branches, being scratched up as you walk through thick brush, and constantly under threat of attack by wild animals. It can help to remember that surviving the walk through the jungle is just an obstacle on the way to achieving the main goal.

Part of learning how to be obedient to God, is learning how to navigate through the jungle, past the obstacles. It can help your mindset a great deal, if you remember we are on the team of the main character and, like the movies, our side wins in the end. We just have to follow His lead, and He will guide us to the treasure that awaits. In fact, the more closely you stick to Jesus, the more clearly you can see Him ahead of you on the path. He is removing the obstacles before you even encounter them, and keeping the lions, tigers, and bears at bay. We can keep moving forward on our mission, trusting that if we stay right behind Him, the path will be clear. If we veer off the path, however, and try to forge our own way home, we find ourselves in the middle of trouble once again.

As we have seen, obeying God is not always easy. We are asked to step outside of our comfort zones, take risks, and sometimes blindly walk along this path, trusting only God's direction. The tasks He gives us can be time-consuming and challenging enough, just on their own. The tasks become all the more complex when we factor in the enemy, and the distractions and impediments they use to try to stop us from completing them. Distractions come in many different forms, ranging from minor inconveniences, to major setbacks. We learned about trials and temptations in *Pursuit to Commitment*. If we are prepared in advance for these distractions and impediments, we will be much more likely to overcome them, and complete our assignments.

The first, and probably one of the most common, is often called 'imposter syndrome'. Imposter syndrome can happen in any field, especially to those who are new at their career or hobby. If we can feel unqualified to do simple worldly jobs, how much easier is it for us to feel unqualified and unworthy to take on the monumental task of serving God? We already discussed this issue earlier, and learned most of us feel this way.

We can feel like our knowledge and skills are far too basic, and that we could never do what He is asking. We see well-spoken pastors, experts in apologetics, or world-class artists perform, and believe we could never be knowledgeable or talented enough to serve God. We hear professors debate various aspects of the Bible, and worry we are not intelligent enough to serve God. The examples of the 'heroes of the faith' are so huge and daunting, that we can feel like we could never possibly do anything that monumental. As I mentioned earlier, I feel this way often, about writing these books, or about sharing my faith. It was much worse when I first started. I was terrified, but through the years my relationship with the Lord, and my confidence in Him, has grown.

I have learned that as long as I stick to doing what He has asked me to do, I do not have to worry about what happens next. Whether what I do is successful or not, is up to God. If my efforts fail, it is because God wanted them to fail for some important reason. In the Bible, we read several examples of people's efforts seemingly failing. We are blessed to be able to read the Biblical stories with 20/20 hindsight. We get to see how God's plans started, the problems and doubts that arose in the middle of their execution, and finally, how God always works them out for the good. If we are wise, we will pay attention, and benefit by learning from these examples.

When Moses was trying to get Pharaoh to let the Israelites leave Egypt, the Lord deliberately hardened Pharaoh's heart, so that he would not relent and let them go too soon. Yahweh knew that Pharaoh would chase after them, so He waited until He had displayed all of the miracles and signs He planned to display. Without the full line of plagues, we would have missed out on making the connection to how Yahweh used them to prove His power over the false Egyptian gods.

We also see this in Joseph's story. He was given a vision of having power and respect, but in order to reach that position, he had to first be brought low by becoming a slave and a prisoner. Surely, while he spent years sitting forgotten in prison, he must have worried that he had misinterpreted the dream God had given him. What he originally thought would be a blessing of power for himself, turned out to be a blessing that saved his entire family, and many others. What seems like failure at first to us, is often a stepping stone to God's plan for success. Be careful not to disobey God by giving up, before His full plan has come into fruition.

Everyone feels this at some point. From the most famous evangelist, to the unsung missionary, we can all feel worried about the success or failure of our endeavors. We are dealing with powerful spiritual entities, who are battling for our souls. Everyone has doubts sometimes. We know we will face a lot of aggression and apprehension when we attempt to share the news of Jesus. We fear that the atheist will know more than we do, or that our testimony is not special enough to convince anyone to believe. We fear we will stumble over our words, or forget everything we know about the Bible in the heat of the moment.

We must remember Jesus tells us not to worry about what we will say, but to trust and allow the Holy Spirit to speak through us. My relationship with Him has given me the desire to learn, driving me to research the compelling issues of our faith. Anytime I know I will be speaking about God, I pray for the Holy Spirit to give me the words I need, and be my voice. The Holy Spirit fills you with a passion for God. Feed on that passion, and use it to spur your desire to be immersed in God's Word. The more you seek and trust the Lord, the more you will grow.

Even if you reach the 'top' and become a leader in the church, you will still face attacks on your worthiness and qualifications to serve. The enemy is relentless and will attack you right up until the end. Maybe you will be invited to speak at a conference, but get hit with a panic attack the night before, anxious that your presentation is not interesting enough. Maybe someone you respect will give you some constructive criticism, or someone will leave hurtful comments on your video, and your pride will suffer. Just when you start to feel like less of an imposter, you will hear or read something about yourself that shakes you. You are going to be ridiculed, and called every name you can think of, when you start discussing your faith in public.

In order to reach the lost, that means we have to share the news with people who don't already know it. Which means we cannot always be comfortable. We have to be willing to experience discomfort and ridicule for our faith. Look at all of the people in the Bible who experienced disdain from their peers, especially Jesus Himself.

We see another example in 2 Samuel 6:20. There, we learn how King David was sneered at by his wife for embarrassing her. She was upset that he was dancing around 'making a fool of himself' to worship the Lord, because all of her servants and friends could see him. It is no different than now. I used to think people who danced around with their arms raised, praising God, were crazy, but now I do that every single day. I suppose I deserve whatever derision I get, as I probably dished some out myself. Take a brief glance at anyone trying to share the Gospel online, and you will always find several rude comments, laughing emojis, and other forms of mockery.

Another form of distraction is one we mentioned before. This is when we pass up or overlook our daily walk with God, in search of some big, dramatic, 'build an ark' kind of calling. Don't be discouraged if your job seems to be over before it starts. Perhaps He asks you to write a song. It is amazing and it gets played at your church, and eventually ends up on the Christian radio stations. You get excited and think 'this is it!' and get ready for your big time musical ministry, writing more songs. But it all just slowly dies down, and nothing else gets any play, no matter how hard you try.

You might be tempted to think that you have failed, or that you have let God down in some way. What is more likely, is that your short-lived musical career served its purpose (assuming you were obeying God's directives with a pure heart). Your song reached the exact person, or people, it needed to reach. Something in it touched them, in a way that nothing else could, and He did not need that song to go any further. Like Esther, perhaps that one job was enough to accomplish what God wanted done. Or perhaps it was all designed to teach you some sort of lesson. If He does not give you any further orders, you can continue in your daily obedience to the Great Commission, knowing that you have fulfilled that specific assignment.

Disobedience could also involve doing something you were not asked to do. There will sometimes be occasions where God says 'no' before you can even get started. You may think you are doing something positive to share your faith, but then find yourself defeated at every turn. For example, a booth for a Bible-based high school program caught my eye at a festival. I requested information so I could learn about starting groups in my area schools. I got samples of the materials, and figured I would have no problem reaching out to churches and friends, recruiting volunteers. I imagined huge groups, taking over the area, bringing hundreds of teens to Christ. Instead, it was radio silence from everyone I reached out to. Texts and emails went unanswered. No one even turned it down, or said they were too busy. I kept trying different routes, but received literally no response.

I was uncertain whether I should keep trying. Was this the enemy trying to stop me, or was this an indication that God did not want me to pursue that particular path at that particular time? How do you tell the difference between a test that you have to overcome, and God putting obstacles in your path to stop you? Prayer. I prayed and asked Him. I said I was willing to do whatever He wanted me to do. I would either keep moving forward, or give it up, but I needed to know what His will and direction were. I asked Him to have someone reach out to me within a certain amount of time, if He wanted me to keep trying.

To this day, no one has ever contacted me, despite the representatives saying they would follow up. I also completely stopped feeling any sort of urge, or push to continue to pursue this path. Even though I thought I had a great idea, God had other plans. I believe prayer, and reading the Bible, are currently our best ways of knowing God's will. If we always turn to the Lord with our questions, concerns, and problems, He will help us. When we are not sure whether God is preventing us from going down a certain path, or if we just have to persevere and try harder, prayer, and trusting God, will give us the answers we seek.

We have to submit to His will, whatever that may be, even if we think we have a really great idea, because His ways are best. I can only guess at why God did not want me to pursue the youth program. Perhaps the group would have served as a major distraction from the other things He has me focusing on, maybe there was something in the lessons that is inaccurate, or maybe I just was not the right person for the job. Sometimes, we might discover that our ideas or intentions were not so pure after all. For example, in Numbers 22, we see an example of how God warns us when we are doing something we shouldn't be doing.

The king of Moab had sent for the prophet Balaam to come and curse Israel, in the hopes he might be able to defeat them. Balaam was initially told by God to ignore the request, and not to even go to the king. The king pressured Balaam, offering him great rewards, so even though he had already been told no, he inquired of Yahweh again. At that point God told Balaam he could go, but could only speak the words Yahweh gave, and not the curse the king wanted to hear. Along the way, it seems Balaam's motives may have turned to the profit and reward he could get by cursing Israel as the king desired, so God stopped him in his tracks, literally:

> Balaam rose up in the morning, and saddled his donkey, and went with the princes of Moab. God's anger burned because he went; and Yahweh's angel placed himself in the way as an adversary against him. Now he was riding on his donkey, and his two servants were with him. The donkey saw Yahweh's angel standing in the way, with his sword drawn in his hand; and the donkey turned out of the path, and went into the field. Balaam struck the donkey, to turn her into the path. Then Yahweh's angel stood in a narrow path between the vineyards, a wall

> being on this side, and a wall on that side. The donkey saw Yahweh's angel, and she thrust herself to the wall, and crushed Balaam's foot against the wall. He struck her again. Yahweh's angel went further, and stood in a narrow place, where there was no way to turn either to the right hand or to the left. The donkey saw Yahweh's angel, and she lay down under Balaam. Balaam's anger burned, and he struck the donkey with his staff. Yahweh opened the mouth of the donkey, and she said to Balaam, "What have I done to you, that you have struck me these three times?" Balaam said to the donkey, "Because you have mocked me, I wish there were a sword in my hand, for now I would have killed you." The donkey said to Balaam, "Am I not your donkey, on which you have ridden all your life long until today? Was I ever in the habit of doing so to you?" He said, "No." Then Yahweh opened the eyes of Balaam, and he saw Yahweh's angel standing in the way, with his sword drawn in his hand; and he bowed his head, and fell on his face. Yahweh's angel said to him, "Why have you struck your donkey these three times? Behold, I have come out as an adversary, because your way is perverse before me. The donkey saw me, and turned away before me these three times. Unless she had turned away from me, surely now I would have killed you, and saved her alive." Balaam said to Yahweh's angel, "I have sinned; for I didn't know that you stood in the way against me. Now therefore, if it displeases you, I will go back again." Yahweh's angel said to Balaam, "Go with the men; but you shall only speak the word that I shall speak to you." (Numbers 22:21-35)

Once we realize God has put a stumbling block in place, we must give up our own plan, and focus on what He wants us to do instead. We have to realize that just because an idea sounds great to us, He always knows best.

Sometimes the obstacles in your path are not God's way of stopping you, they are placed there by the enemy. In these instances, God expects you to persevere in spite of them. When you pray about them, God will encourage you to push forward, and be persistent. When my first book was published, I had an order from God to mail a copy to at least 100 churches, along with the others we were giving out. I spent hours looking for churches, and finding their addresses to compile a mailing list. I wrote and printed out letters to send with the books. At first, I purchased envelopes that were too small. When I purchased the correct size, stuffed them, addressed them, and went to mail them, I found out I could really only send off about ten at a time, without completely holding up the line at the post office. I had to take them in a little bit at a time, and spread the job out to a few different post offices.

Once they were all ready to be mailed, I was relieved and thought that was it. Unfortunately, it began to seem like every time I mailed out a batch, one or two would get returned. I felt like I was never going to be able to mail all of them out. I'd check and correct the addresses, or choose a different place to send them. I spent so much time back and forth at the post office, until, finally, I put the last book in the mail.

It had been over two weeks with nothing returned, so I assumed everything was good. One hundred books sent! Then I checked my mail. You guessed it, there was yet another returned book waiting for me! I was so frustrated. I left the book sitting by my bed for a while, wondering why it was so difficult to finish mailing all of the books. I was resenting this task, not doing well emotionally, because I was not trusting God. Sending out 99 books was not enough. I knew if I didn't get the 100th book sent out to the 100th church, I would be disobeying God. Finally, I forced myself to get it together, found an address for a different church, and sent it off.

The next night, after completing my task, God told me to check my email. I almost didn't listen, because I had been compulsively checking it, and was trying to cut back. I expected to see a message from a church requesting books, or seeking more information. I was absolutely shocked to see an email from the local Christian radio station, inviting me to appear on a popular show to discuss the book! The host of the show focuses on religion and politics, and he is somewhat of a household name in the metro-Detroit area. I do not believe I would have been given that opportunity, had I left that last envelope laying there, and quit at book 99. It was a sign to me that God saw my obedience (and lack thereof).

This was my first-ever radio appearance, and I was excited, but extremely nervous. As previously mentioned, I had a fear of speaking on this topic. I had no idea what questions would be asked, or how I would possibly answer them, so I prayed beforehand for the Holy Spirit to take over. When it was finished, I was sweaty, and could not really recall much of what I said. I felt like I survived, flustering a lot, but not totally bombing.

I realized a few days later that I was overly worried about how I came across. While part of me was nervous about representing God's Word correctly, and doing well by Him, there was also a rather large part of me that was insecure about what my friends, family, the host, and his listeners would think of me. I was letting my fear over their judgment affect my service to God. If God can make a nobody like me write a book, and go on the radio, it is surely even more proof that He can do anything. I learned we can be bold in our faith, so long as we completely give up control of ourselves to Him. He proved that my frustration and complaints were completely without merit. I had to learn to trust Him completely. It did not matter how well I spoke, or really even what I said. What mattered is that I obeyed Him. My pride and fear could have easily taken hold, and deterred me from completing my assignment.

Usually, distractions are not one major event, they are the little things that add up. Work and life problems get in the way of our obedience to the work God has called us to do. Small problems, like drama with a coworker, or an argument with our spouse, can have us turning back to our old crutches, rather than seeking God. Bigger events, like a debilitating injury, or getting divorced, can easily distract us for years. If we waste time sulking, gossiping, or drowning our sorrows in wine and chocolate, we are forgetting, just like many biblical figures, that we should always seek comfort from God in our times of need. When we seek comfort in our guilty pleasures, we step off the path of obedience, and we delay our progress.

If we aren't careful to snap back to reality, and return our focus to the Lord, we could even find ourselves giving up on our tasks permanently. We must remain alert to the distractions, and practice pulling our mind and heart back to Him. We can do this by taking a moment to close our eyes, breathe deeply, and talk to God, every time we find ourselves distracted. Tell Him that you are struggling, scared, angry, overwhelmed, or whatever it is you are feeling. Ask Him for His help to overcome, and to find peace in the chaos. Keep praying until you feel your focus returning. Ask Him to help you stay on track, and be obedient.

God reminded me, when I was having a day filled with panic attacks and tearfulness, that all of the crazy awful, good, bad, and in between things that happen in my life, are merely distractions. They are designed to try to keep me from doing the work He has asked me to do. I do not know how or when His plans will come into fruition, but He has shown me time and again that I can trust Him. I just need to keep my eyes fixed on Him, and continue to move in obedience. He will handle everything else. My job is to keep practicing the spiritual disciplines, and be obedient to His commands. If I do so, everything else will 'fall into place' exactly how He intends.

No matter how difficult obedience is, we must obey. Sometimes the tasks will be so harrowing, that we really do not want to have to even think about them, let alone face them head on. We might be tempted to seek our own will, and ask God to find another job for us, or a different way to accomplish His plans. Even Jesus felt that anguish as He was preparing to go to the cross, but through that process, He showed us the ultimate lesson in obeying God's orders. We can learn so much from Jesus as he prayed, saying, "Now my soul is troubled. What shall I say? 'Father, save me from this time'? But I came to this time for this cause. Father, glorify your name!" Though He greatly desired not to have to suffer torture and death, He knew that this was the very reason God sent Him. Our tasks might seem troubling and difficult, but we must reject and turn away from our fear and dread, and turn toward His calling.

NOTES

9

THE END

Teach me your way, Yahweh. I will walk in your truth. Make my heart undivided to fear your name. I will praise you, Lord my God, with my whole heart. I will glorify your name forever more.

- Psalm 86:11-12

Let your eyes look straight ahead. Fix your gaze directly before you. Make the path of your feet level. Let all of your ways be established. Don't turn to the right hand nor to the left. Remove your foot from evil.

- Proverbs 4:25-27

Therefore don't throw away your boldness, which has a great reward. For you need endurance so that, having done the will of God, you may receive the promise.

- Hebrews 10:35-36

God wants you. He wants you to be a laborer working on His harvest. If you build your relationship with Him, and communicate daily, when the time comes, you will know if there is something specific He wants you to do. He never forces us to do what He asks, although He may *strongly* encourage us. He gives us time to make the right choice. He has been very patient, allowing us the opportunity to repent from our sinful ways, and return to Him, but soon enough, our time will be up. We have the choice of how we spend what remains of our time. Will we walk with the Lord every day, obedient to His will, or will we keep one foot in this world, resisting what we know He wants us to do?

As I said at the start of this book, we must seek the Lord, know the Lord, and share the Lord. If we do those things every day, with a heart full of love for God and people, then we will surely not stumble. It is only when we try to deviate from the Lord, that we find ourselves uncertain, or in trouble. I have used the analogy of the old cartoons with a devil on one shoulder, and an angel on the other, each trying to convince the character to do things their way. That basically sums up our daily requirement to be obedient to Yahweh, in every single choice we make. We must choose to listen to His voice every time. Literally.

However, right now we live in a place where the angels on our shoulders are drowned out by the devil's loud voice. Our world is the way it is because of the dominance of the devils on our shoulders. We are so easily manipulated and swayed by their wicked advice, that we do not even bother to consult with the angel on the other side. People constantly live in torment because they, and everyone around them, are mainly concerned with their own selfish desires. As we know, these desires can never be satisfied, so we are always yearning, angry, bitter, and resentful. We search for more, and never find enough. Agony, and the absence of goodness, is what you will live in, if you are unwilling to brush the evil voice off your shoulder, and focus only on the voice of good. Kick the devil out, and only allow goodness to fill your mind and heart.

We must be at peace, knowing that God is in control, and we must be still, listening quietly and carefully for the small whisper of His direction. We must build our relationship with Him, so that we can know and distinguish the call of His voice, and discern the pull of the Holy Spirit guiding our conscience. We must keep our focus on His Word, through daily, constant reading of the Bible, and prayer. We must pray for patience and wisdom to trust in, and understand, God's will.

The answer to each and every question, the only way to know exactly what to do in every situation, is to be legitimately praying without ceasing, and listening to the voice of Our Father. You must have a strong, committed relationship with Him. This happens when you are filled with the Holy Spirit, and stay continually focused on the Lord, and His next instruction. Before you make a move, or decide on a course of action, consult with God first. Ask Him if it is a good idea, and then humbly obey whatever He says, without question or delay. Follow God, walk in the Way, the Truth, and the Life of Jesus.

Glorify God by living in daily obedience to Him. Truly live within Christ, and invite Him to abide in you. Embrace the Holy Spirit's correction and guidance. Allow Him to help you, so that you can help other people find God. Allow yourself to be changed, so that you can go out and be the change this world needs. Share your testimony of what He has done in your life. Listen to the directions God gives you, and obey His commands. This is how you will bear fruit. This is how you will play a role in bringing your brothers and sisters to His eternal kingdom. This is how you become a new creation. This is how your life, and the world, changes for the good.

Most gracious and merciful Father,
You have given us so much to be thankful for, and provided us with so many opportunities to help grow Your kingdom, through sharing the news of salvation with our brothers and sisters. Please give us the courage to obey Your calling, and to take risks to advance Your name, not our own. We come to You humbly, and fully submitted to Your will. Please make it known to us, and help us to live according to Your will, so that our lives may be examples of Your light and love to the rest of the world. Help us to glorify Your mighty name, through our faithful obedience to Your will.
Amen.

APPENDIX

Below you will find a link, as well as some QR codes, that will take you to a few of the conversations I have had with atheists online. Simply type the link into your browser, take a picture of the codes with your phone, or scan them with a QR reader app, and click the link. The conversations are sometimes in the comments, so you may have to scroll to the comments section, look for my name, and click to read them. Feel free to join in and add what I missed, or start some discussions of your own! The more workers in the field, the greater the harvest!

https://www.quora.com/profile/Elizabeth-Napier-15

https://www.quora.com/Is
-there-scientific-evidenc...

https://www.quora.com
/Where-did-the-biblica...

About the Author

Elizabeth was a sinner, turned child of God, who is on a mission to share the good news of our salvation through Jesus Christ. She writes books in obedience to God's will, praying that they will help others seek God. She lives a simple life in Michigan with her family, and has had careers as both a lawyer and teacher. She believes all honor and glory are reserved for the Lord, and seeks to love God and love people in accordance with His commandments. She welcomes you to email her at savedsisterinchrist@gmail.com if you have any questions about your personal journey.

<u>Books in the Logic to Rest series</u>:
Logic to Belief
Belief to Pursuit
Pursuit to Commitment
Commitment to Obedience
Obedience to Rest (coming 2025)

Made in the USA
Middletown, DE
10 January 2025